ZODIAC

WILTSHIRE

Edited by Donna Samworth

First published in Great Britain in 2002 by
YOUNG WRITERS
Remus House,
Coltsfoot Drive,
Peterborough, PE2 9JX
Telephone (01733) 890066

HB ISBN 0 75433 702 2
SB ISBN 0 75433 703 0

Foreword

Young Writers was established in 1991 with the aim of promoting creative writing in children, to make reading and writing poetry fun.

Once again, this year proved to be a tremendous success with over 41,000 entries received nationwide.

The Zodiac competition has shown us the high standard of work and effort that children are capable of today. The competition has given us a vivid insight into the thoughts and experiences of today's younger generation. It is a reflection of the enthusiasm and creativity that teachers have injected into their pupils, and it shines clearly within this anthology.

The task of selecting poems was a difficult one, but nevertheless, an enjoyable experience. We hope you are as pleased with the final selection in *Zodiac Wiltshire* as we are.

CONTENTS

The Poems

The Teenage Years

They act like they just don't care,
Even though they do,
They argue over what to wear
And then they yell at you!

Their expression only changes,
When they are with their friends,
But with their family it is all the same,
God, will it never end?

Why don't they ever listen
And just take others' advice?
Why don't they smile for a start
Or just try being nice?

Why do they try to be so difficult?
For they make other lives so hard,
Why? Emotions are torn
But when they emerge from adolescents,
Their attitude is reborn!

I do not claim that I am perfect,
For no person can ever be,
But the teenage years protrude
Notorious for being rude
And though they cause much strife,
Those years will always be seen,
As the defiant part of life!

Ollie Callaway (13)

Horoscopes

Twins and scorpions, what can they mean?
Astrologers think they can see the unseen,
It's written in the stars, or so they say,
It's written in the papers every day,
Some people believe, others don't.
Some take the advice, others won't,
The stars rule our lives, some believe,
Are they there to help or do they deceive?
The stars, the moon and the sun,
Some take it seriously, others for fun,
Your birth date shows what you are,
A sheep or fish, the answer's not far,
In our lives they can be nothing or everything,
They can be anything or something,
So, what's your star sign?

Sarah-Jane McAlpine (11)
Abbeyfield School

Midnight Moon

A full moon glows in the sky
And clouds drift slowly by,
It's midnight and everything is calm,
A gentle breeze and rustling trees,
Small animals scamper around in the grass,
It's midnight, everything is calm within the
Light of the moon.

Damon Fletcher (11)
Abbeyfield School

Spells

Wizards, witches,
Frogs and toads,
Magic spells,
Nobody knows.

Rats and mice,
Toads and frogs,
Magic spells
Who knows.

Cloaks and hats,
Flying broomsticks,
Magic spells,
I know!

Dan Boulton (11)
Abbeyfield School

Autumn's Here At Last

The golden leaves are falling,
While the waking sun is dawning,
Autumn's here at last.

The trees are standing bare,
There's a stillness in the air,
Autumn's here at last.

The air is crisp and still,
With a warm refreshing chill,
Autumn's here at last.

Flo Sanders (12)
Abbeyfield School

THE NO HOPE SCHOOL - FOR THE GIFTED

After dropping my mum off at playgroup
I drove to school.
In English I taught the teachers how to divide
I thought they'd never learn!
Mr Swot got a detention
He got full marks in the spelling test.
Mrs Spellwell was the star pupil
She refused to do the spelling test.
The deputy head had to clean the cafeteria
He started a food fight with the head, Mr Alwaysright.
Mr Mumble and Mr Grace joined Mr Swot in detention
They were fighting in the playground.
PE was awful!
Mr Nifty got stuck at the bottom of the climbing frame.
I had to go up and get him.
The science corridor is out of bounds
Mr Banga, the science teacher's experiment went a bit wrong.
At home time, the teachers' parents collected them,
I was left to plan tomorrow's lessons for these top pupils.

Claire Selman (11)
Abbeyfield School

THE HOOVER

Hoover, Hoover going round,
Making such a funny sound,
Sucking up what's on the ground,
Hoover, Hoover going round.
Please try not to make a sound,
Cleaning everything that's on the ground.

Tom Grimshaw (13)
Abbeyfield School

Scorpio

Scorpio is burning
Like a raging fire
My flames are high, they reach up to the sky,
Like my tail as you pass me by.
Scorpio is burning
Like a vibrant flame,
I'm so exciting,
But beware of my sting.
Scorpio is burning
Like a violent torch,
You look at me there with my power and force,
Which leads me through my exciting course,
Scorpio is burning
Like a crackling fire,
I'm forceful and powerful,
Enter my power,
Scorpio will burn in the night sky,
With my powerful excitement
It will thrill you forever.

Stacey Vincent (11)
Abbeyfield School

My Friend Billy

My best friend's name was Billy,
He was born ever so silly,
He blew up a bomb
And everything had gone
And that was the end of silly Billy.

Jack Woollings (11)
Abbeyfield School

FOOTBALL

A player was going to say
Move out of my way
He was going for goal
He fell down a hole
He got the ball
Then he did fall
He got a red card
This he found hard
He scored a goal
So he did a roll
The crowd roared
The referee was bored
The ball's on the spot
The players are hot
The game was over
They drove back to Dover.

James Ellis (12)
Abbeyfield School

I'M THINKING

A poem I was asked to write,
Came as a bit of a fright,
I wondered what I could say,
I jumbled words in any way.
My endings I tried to rhyme,
But I didn't seem to have the time.
So I've written these words for you
I very much hope that they will do?

Cassian M Edwards (11)
Abbeyfield School

Sagittarius

The great horse archer
Up on high
Watching over the whole sky
Wherever evil may appear
You can bet he is here

Watching over
Flying high
Ever in the black chill sky
Riding this way
Maybe that
Sweeping silently as a cat

Looking at
The archer centaur
Thinking if he is a mentor
Across the sky from east to west
The greatest . . .
Sagittarius the arching centaur.

Ben Gray (12)
Abbeyfield School

Autumn Trees

It's the time of year when the trees turn red,
Branches sway around in the autumn breeze,
The leaves go to and fro as they fall to the ground,
You would think the trees were dead,
But they are in a deep, deep sleep.

Thomas C Tweedale (11)
Abbeyfield School

My Morning - Oh No!

School can be good,
School can be bad,
When school is over,
I am really glad.

At 7am, I am woken by my light,
My mum must have had a miserable night,
I go to the bathroom to wash and clean,
John's used all the toothpaste,
He is so mean.

Mum has had her coffee
She has calmed down
John is doing breakfast
But the toast is too brown.

The time is 7.30
The doorbell rings,
It's my friend Nat
And I let her in.

We have time to wait
Because John is so late,
I bet he has stopped for a paper
And that I so hate.

He drops us off on his way
Never mind it's just another day . . .

Kerry Summers (11)
Abbeyfield School

Two Towers, Two Planes

It is the morning, in an airport rush, people phoning and in a crush.
A window seat and no smoking please, your bags are checked,
Your tickets please.

In New York the streets are alive, people walking to work,
some that drive.
The sun is shining, the sky is blue, the World Trade Center,
I've got work to do.

Seat belts on, the cabin lights say, seats up, right we're on our way,
The sun is shining, the sky is blue,
The terrorists are thinking what they're about to do.

The plane is up high, the sun is so bright,
The terrorists take over, this can't be right.
The plane banks left, New York's up ahead,
The Twin Towers are looming and soon we'll be dead.

Two towers, two planes, the 11th September
Soon to become a day to remember,
One plane, one tower and then the other,
People jumping and screaming and holding each other.

The world watches the planes hit the Twin Towers,
It's shown over and over on TV for hours.
One month on, the sun is still shining,
The sky is still blue, the Twin Towers are still burning.
What should we do?

Daniel Collard (12)
Abbeyfield School

SPRING

Spring
Spring is best,
It's a time to rest
Under a tree,
Happy as can be,
Baby animals are born,
Spring is fun.

Summer
Summer is hot,
Like a boiling pot,
Birds are singing in the trees,
Bees are flying in the air,
A breeze is dancing in my hair.

Autumn
Autumn is full of colour,
Brown, red, yellow, orange,
Autumn is crunch! Crunch! Crunch!
Through the leaves.

Winter
Winter is cold,
It's a time to build snowmen,
In your house you have a roaring fire,
The snow is getting higher.

Ashleigh Male (11)
Abbeyfield School

MY HALLOWE'EN POEM

People say 'Trick or treat,'
But they don't come out all neat,
When they all come out at night,
Trying to give someone a fright.

Witches fly up in the sky,
On their brooms as they fly,
Ghosts and ghouls come walking out,
So be very careful with what you shout.

Simon Winterbottom (11)
Abbeyfield School

The Name We Dare Not Speak

In a dark, misty, haunted cemetery,
Stood a girl, a girl with a horrifying past.
Her name we dare not speak is Mary Crawford until
she existed no more.
Whenever a person crosses the cemetery,
they never come back.

This is what happened.
What happened to the girl with a horrifying past,
Nobody goes there now because your flesh is ripped from you
limb by limb.
Because it is haunted,
Haunted by the girl with a horrifying past.

Nobody was there to mourn the girl,
They thought that she was a nuisance.
So there was no funeral for the girl who had her life cut short.
She was just dumped to lie in her rotting coffin forever.
The girl with a horrifying past.

She went missing, nobody found her alive.
They found her head buried in the soil,
Near to her mother's grave.
They only found segments, segments of her battered body.

Victoria Sage (12)
Abbeyfield School

Hallowe'en The Scream

The street is gleaming
With pumpkins all bright,
The children all screaming into the night,
Running round with witches' hats and Devil's horns,
Their bags all filled with treats so yummy
That they're sure to fill your tummy.
Skeletons and ghosts are haunting the place,
Make sure not to stare them right in the face.
Vampires wearing their cloaks
And their sharp blood-gleaming teeth.
For tonight is Hallowe'en,
The time for trick or treat.

Stephen Pearce (11)
Abbeyfield School

Taurus The Bull

Taurus the bull was feeling rather full
After eating four sheep and a donkey.
He lay on the floor, then wanted some more
But couldn't get up because he was wonky.
So he shouted for help and gave out a yelp,
When he saw a crab coming towards him.
The crab pinched his nose and Taurus he rose,
Off the floor and he felt rather slim.
He looked at the crab and gave him a jab
And the crab rolled under a stone.
The bull licked his lips and wiggled his hips,
Then swallowed them both with a groan.

Sarah Tully (11)
Abbeyfield School

GEMINI

Gemini's sign is the twins,
They can have terrible sins,
Sometimes nice, kind and helpful,
Other times horrible, selfish and spiteful.

With birthdays between 22nd of May and 21st June,
Some Geminis act like a goon,
Some don't get up till noon,
Some can even play a tune.

They have split personalities,
They even have exceptionalities
Especially on what they say
And when they try to get their own way.

Hannah Wilkins (13)
Abbeyfield School

AUTUMN

Autumn is crisp,
Autumn smells new,
Autumn's grass is painted with dew.

Autumn is fresh,
Crunchy leaves on the ground,
Blackberries and apples are there to be found.

The flowers have faded,
The berries are red,
Thoughts of ghosts swirl round my head.

Ian Wood (11)
Abbeyfield School

My School Day

Wakey wakey, my day's begun,
It's breakfast time, I fill my tum,
Once washed and dressed,
I check I'm wearing my winter vest,
The walk to school is a chore
And what's more there's more to endure.
The bell rings, time for lunch,
We gather round in a hungry bunch,
After lunch, we have PE,
Oh no today it's hockey.
Now the school day is complete
I'll walk home, then rest my feet.

Claire Martin (11)
Abbeyfield School

My Family

My dad likes to collect things,
From tennis rackets to old rings.

My mum hates cleaning the house,
Especially when she sees a mouse.

My brother makes lots of noise,
When he's playing with his toys.

My sister is always on the phone,
Talking to her friend Simone.

Last of all there's me,
I'm pretty normal as you can see!

Aimee Williams (11)
Abbeyfield School

THE ZODIAC - VIRGO

I am a Virgo and I'm very proud
All my friends say I'm very loud,
Even though the stars say that I'm shy,
I really, really don't know why.

I'm persevering in carrying out tasks,
To the bitter end as long as they last,
In precise detail I will explore
Until I cannot explore anymore.

I think that zodiacs can be cool
And sometimes they really rule!
I'm not too sure if the zodiac is true
Sometimes I don't believe, but sometimes I do!

Natasha Townsend (12)
Abbeyfield School

CHRISTMAS

Autumn passes as winter comes near,
As Christmas trees suddenly appear.
Cold damp nights,
With very bright lights,
Glowing in the winter sky.
Children writing for lots of toys,
Some from girls and some from boys,
Rudolph's nose is bright red,
Stockings hanging on your bed,
Santa's coming,
So get to sleep,
Then you'll find all your treats.

Amy Skudder (11)
Abbeyfield School

Four Seasons

Yellow flowers are blooming,
Trumpets nod their heads,
A dazzling, shiny pillow.

The holidays are coming,
Beach and deep blue sea,
Fields showing sheets of colour.

Orange and yellow floating,
Softly to the ground,
A multicoloured carpet.

White rain has started falling,
It is getting cold,
A white blanket covers the roofs.

Jonathan Alder (12)
Abbeyfield School

Taurus The Bull

Mighty and steadfast in the face of danger
Strong, fast to those who he deems worthy of protection
Kind and gentle to those of pure heart
Tolerant, patient to those who oppose the oppressive
Are the virtues of the bull
When I met it staring straight into those eyes
Eyes alone defeated me
But then I saw compassion, pity even love
In this lord of beasts was love
The bull
Lord.

Neil Tucker (12)
Abbeyfield School

STARS

It's good being a bright sparkling star
You shine so beautifully, high in the dark sky
Even though we don't wear uniforms or ties
When we're eating gigantic pies.

It's brilliant being a glittering star
You reflect off the large monkey bars,
Which are fixed firmly to the bumpy black tar
This is to prevent you from driving fast in a car.

It's great being a reflecting star
Your patterns go very, very far
Even to the colour cars,
Which are next to the monkey bars.

Kerry-Ann Hammond (11)
Abbeyfield School

PISCES - THE FISH

He swims gracefully through the deep
waters of the long lake,
Never emerging to human eyes,
Always confined to his underwater palace,
Yet he still has the power to bless the children
who fall prisoner to his time.
He occasionally meets with his fellow zodiacs
in the stars to discuss important matters,
Then he goes for a nice relaxing swim,
To wear off all troubling subjects.
Still not emerging to human eyes.

Liam Walker (12)
Abbeyfield School

STARLIGHT

When the light
Ceases to glow
It gives some people a fright,
Because they don't know,
The stars are looking down on them.

Starlight, a wonderful thing,
Look out your window, you'll definitely see,
The amazing glow, then you'll sing
Stars please shine on me.

Every night
Stars shine their light
Brightening up the people with fright
And so I write.

When the light
Ceases to glow
It gives some people a fright,
Because they don't know
The stars are looking down on them.

Jamie Rimmer (11)
Abbeyfield School

MY JUMPER

Today my jumper came through the post,
It's the gift I really wanted most,
The sleeves are the colour of lime green,
It's the best jumper I've ever seen.
The colour of the collar's rosy red,
I'm really sure that I'll sleep with it in bed.

Zurain Qureshi (11)
Abbeyfield School

I Went To Town

There was one day, when I went to town,
To pick up a pair of shoes,
I went to the shop man
And gave him a shotgun,
Then there was nothing to lose.

I could take all the shoes I wanted
Because the shop man was dead on the floor,
But I only needed one pair
So I gave some to the neighbour next door.

The police knocked at my door,
But I could tell them no more,
Other than try the neighbour next door,
But when they knocked at his door,
They saw some other new shoes on the floor,
So their opinions soon changed
And now the man lives there, no more!

Jake McMillan (11)
Abbeyfield School

Hope

If it rains
Or hails,
Or snows
And all else fails,
Then at least you still have a fire,
Where you may retire,
To warmth.

Simon Corke (11)
Abbeyfield School

The Elements

The furnace of flame whose ability to mame
Is greater than that of the rest - can keep one's heart
Warm with shelter from the winterness.

The block of winter, the torrent of rain, the staple
Drink of life with none. Death gave a star the vital
Element, remember this water is life.

The beam of wind, the blade of cold.
For air is making of old and all next
To no mass makes this element
Gold like water. It is life.

The boulder of dirt, earth and stone
It is mass, itself and nothing is complete
Without it. Is Earth, the planet, the universe
For this is the final verse.

Matthew Falconer (11)
Abbeyfield School

Monsters

Monsters are not sweet,
It's horrible what they eat,
They're hairy, they're scary,
Some have smelly feet,
They scare you in the night,
Where there's not any light,
Some are tall, some are small
And some are really cruel!

Amber Carter (12)
Abbeyfield School

ARIES

From the
21st March to the 20th April,
The star sign Aries roams,
My star sign says I'm meant to be
Confident and quick,
Normally I'm just like a fox!
Sly and secretive,
Obviously they don't know me,
For what I really am.

The animal, the ram
Symbolises this star sign
Because they're just like me
Quick and confident,
That's how we all should be.

Daisy Garraway (11)
Abbeyfield School

FISHING

Fishing
An old sport,
Fun, exciting, adventurous,
Like a blast of excitement,
When you get a bite,
Like a present when you bring it in,
It makes me feel happy and glad,
I feel like a ball of joy waiting to explode
Fishing,
Reminds us about the wonderful fish in the water.

Ben Goulding (11)
Abbeyfield School

SEARCHING

As I wander through the stars
Admiring Saturn, Pluto and Mars
Through timeless ages
Like the turning of pages
I search for the signs of the future.

Aquarius, essential to all life
Helps thirsty soldiers
In their moments of strife

Gemini are twins
Who live as one
For them the
Future has never begun

Aries is a bad-tempered ram
But he will travel to God
Like a gentle lamb

Leo is a lion
Who guards the night
For his people he will fight

Libra are the scales who
Balance out life to make all things equal
So there is no conflict between God's people

Scorpio is the scorpion
Who will sting and fight
He will provide you with a guiding light

Taurus is the bull
Who is stubborn and strong
He will protect you all day long

Pisces are the fish
Who are sensitive and kind
The future they will help you find

Cancer the crab
Will help you find a love that's true
Certain to last a lifetime through

Capricorn is the goat
Who will help you find
Patience in life and peace of mind

Sagittarius is the archer
Who is brave and strong
He will watch over you all night long

Virgo is the virgin
Who watches you with a close eye
To make sure you tell the truth and not a lie

All these signs are the future
I can see
The future is the Earth
And the Earth is *me.*

Michelle Carr (12)
Abbeyfield School

MY HARVEST POEM

H is for herons that fly all around,
A is for autumn colours that spread on the ground.
R is for rabbits that run through the woods,
V is for vegetables that do us all good,
E is for everyone rehearsing their play,
S is for swans that glide a long way,
T hat spells harvest.

Sebastian Murray (12)
Abbeyfield School

STARS

When I look up at the stars,
I see my star sign away so far.

When I see the dark, gloomy sky,
A glittering star catches my eye.

The stars are up at a massive height,
But they still are a wonderful sight.

Sometimes I wish that I could fly,
So I could be with those beautiful stars up high.

Those stars they brighten up the night,
With their bright, dazzling, gleaming sight.

I reach my hand up high and far,
But I cannot catch that delightful star!

Emma Millard (11)
Abbeyfield School

VIRGO

The Virgo lady is modest and shy,
Meticulous and reliable,
Practical and diligent,
Intelligent and analytical.

But on the dark side . . .

Fussy and a worrier,
Overcritical and harsh,
Perfectionist and conservative.

Elizabeth Morgan (13)
Abbeyfield School

THE ZODIAC

When I look into the sky,
The stars are somewhat hard to see,
Huge round balls of stars fly by
Which star sign is for me?

Scorpio and Cancer
October and July,
Looking at the stars bright flow,
In the silky sky.

Look at Leo in the sky,
It seems so still I wonder why
Will the stars ever come back?
Come back as the zodiac.

Michael Whytock (12)
Abbeyfield School

ARIES

I am Aries, as quick and as speedy
As a cheetah in the hot deserts.
Strong of mind and strong of body.
I warn off evil spirits from the dark shadows
And banish them into oblivion.
I am trustworthy and loyal,
A keeper of secrets.
I am as strong as I look
With my big horns and beady eyes.

Jason Shepherd (12)
Abbeyfield School

My Zodiac Poems

Leo the lion is my star sign
And the legend says the lion, is made of pine,
It makes me alive and helps me think clear.

The sign of my birth,
With words that sum up my day,
Which if you don't read,
You might have to pay.

Cancer the crab is always a nag,
He should be kept in a bag,
With lots of rags.
They come in flocks
And swim in the docks
And even wear socks.

Pisces the fish had a wish
In a breakfast dish,
They live in ponds
And appear from words,
They're all different colours
From all different families,
That all eat cranberries.

Amy Sheppard (11)
Abbeyfield School

Keith And The Kangaroo

There once was a young man called Keith,
Who went to the country beneath,
He met a kangaroo
When he went to the loo
And it punched him from here to Clonleth.

Sam Miller (11)
Abbeyfield School

THE ZODIAC

The zodiac is a mysterious place,
Full of wonder and delight.
It has been made from fine lace,
Covering over a blank, surreal darkness.

The empty caverns of nothingness,
The patterns in the sky,
Shining upon us nightly,
From way up high.

Everyone has their own
Special group of stars.
Floating up above,
Bringing all and sundry,
Pure, eternal love.

The zodiac will stretch,
Above, along, beyond.
Waiting for us
In its vague and unearthly etch,
Of forever.

Amy Williams (12)
Abbeyfield School

WE CANCER

C hallenging and creative is Cancer,
A dventurous and amazing are us,
N aughty but neat,
C reepy that's what you can't beat.
E ducational but not equal that's what we are,
R eceptive, that's what makes us beat the rest.

Simone Foster (12)
Abbeyfield School

ME, MYSELF . . . (PISCES)

I am not what I am
A fish swimming,
Glistening like some pebbles
Just drawn from a pond.
Flapping my tail
Really I'm stamping my foot,
With anxiety
To see if that rumour was really true,
To catch up with all the latest gossip
Like I do.
Being a sensitive Piscean soul I am not usually attracted
To those cheeky chaps,
But this boy is supposed to be extra special,
More interesting? . . .
My foot!
A relationship is supposed to crop up this fortnight
Am I supposed to be in *lurve?*
But I am supposed to have a problem,
My friend's secret.
I'm not supposed to tell anyone
But I can't help it,
I need to tell someone this secret.
It's just too much,
This definitely is like me,
Needing to tell someone a
Big,
Huge,
Mighty secret when I promised not to.
I need to,
I want to,
I can't!

Hannah Hugglestone (12)
Abbeyfield School

RACE OF THE STARS

Sagittarius and Capricorn
Are lining up, they're fit but far too cold
Snow will cover their freezing faces
Ice will numb their shaking legs.
Aquarius and Pisces
The best friendship in this race
But you see the look of hatred and envy
As spring never quite reaches them.
Aries and Taurus
Too quiet and shy, yet stubborn
They will run into Gemini for sure
Gemini, those cheats of course
Will sometimes be quite sly
To hitch a ride on a secret star
To reach the Pluto finishing line
Cancer will realise their devious plan
And will try to tell Leo the news
But Leo far away in another universe
Will just stand there brushing her beautiful hair
Virgo is tremendously tall but slow
Though her confidence screams through
She will take on Libra any day
Except Libra wows the men with her fabulous face
She will surely get a quick lead when Mars lets her pass
But finally my Scorpio is the weirdest of them all
She represents everyone whether short or fat or thin
She may not win the race but at least she took part
And all the stars celebrate her
On Fireworks night, November 5th.

Helen Rawlings (12)
Abbeyfield School

WHERE IS IT?

Zodiac, Detonator, Vortex,
Spine-chilling!
Tidal Wave, Logger's Leap, Thunder River,
White knuckle,
Electrifying, exhilarating, enthralling
Where is it?
X:/ No way out, Calgary's Stampede,
Flying fish,
Worth a visit!
Pirates 4D, Depth Charge, Teacup Twisters,
Really cool,
Zodiac, cool, Detonator, thrilling, Vortex,
intense.
Thorpe Park!

Noel Hiorns (11)
Abbeyfield School

FAMILY STAR SIGNS

My dad is a Scorpio, my sister is too,
They're loyal, kind and trustworthy,
But they use their stings a lot too!

My mum is Capricorn, she's really, really kind,
Even when I cut my hand,
She actually didn't mind!

I am Taurus, I'm cool, placid and positive,
I simply am the best,
I always come out on top
And I always beat the rest!

Nicholas West (11)
Abbeyfield School

ZODIAC

Leo the lion is my star sign
But many of you do not have mine
Leo the lion is cunning and strong
He makes you want to sing along.

Cancer the crab is really snippy
Sometimes she can be really lippy
She plays with rocks and hides in docks
Whatever next, will she play in a box?

Virgo the girl is very small
What a shame she isn't tall
She plays outside and makes a sound
Whilst her mum lies in her lounge.

Harriet Easton (12)
Abbeyfield School

FRIENDS

They'll always be there for you
When you are down
Boy problems
Or not going into town
Share secrets
That will never be told
Be friends forever
Young or old
They'll stand by you
Win or lose
Best friends, no friends?
I know which one I would choose!

Heather Candlish (13)
Abbeyfield School

Capricorn Is A Goat

A goat is
Powerful spiralling horns,
Tiny fluffy tail,
Little fuzzy beard,
A baby pink nose,
Enormous bucking hooves,
With attitude!

Faye Allison (11)
Abbeyfield School

Zodiac

The signs of the zodiac are scattered in the sky,
Mapping our fortunes as they watch from on high,
From Aquarius to Capricorn all year through,
They are checking to see if their
Predictions are true.

Devon Wilkins (11)
Abbeyfield School

Schooldays

The outstanding pupils come to play
When they're about, we have a great day,
We thank the teachers for their brilliant teaching,
The enormous school were all preaching.
The yummy food won't make us thin,
But we can work it off in the massive gym,
We start school at half-past eight,
If we get up early, we're never late!

Lauren Grant (11)
Abbeyfield School

CAPRICORN

Splashing, diving, swimming
Running, bouncing, sprinting
Flying, galloping across the space
Guardian of January, power of Saturn
Now is the time of birth, give him your
Blessing, know the time has come
Then speed on round the solar system
Once again

The sun will shine and the rain will fall
The snow will once again come, the time to act is
Here again, time to be the one, the chosen one.
Then speed round the solar system once again
Capricorn.

Richard Graves (12)
Abbeyfield School

THE GRAVEYARD

At night in the graveyard,
Nothing makes a sound.
The ghosts come out,
To haunt the neighbourhood.
As the night grows on,
The ghosts roam the streets,
Looking for people to haunt.
When the sun starts to rise,
The ghosts go back to their graves.
When morning is here,
The graveyard is silent.

Natasha Green (12)
Abbeyfield School

FISHING

It is a full moon,
I can hear the wind rustling through the leaves,
The rain gently patting against the ground,
Whilst I am lying in my bed waiting,
Waiting for the fish to take my bait,
My body is trembling with excitement,
Wow! Something has taken the bait,
It must be at least 30 pounds,
Now the battle begins . . .

Stevie James Blake (11)
Abbeyfield School

VIRGO POEM

I am a Virgo boy,
I can be very timid,
Unless someone makes me livid,
I can be very busy,
I can be very silly,
Virgo boys can also be coy,
They also can be diligent,
Hardworking, persistent boys,
I like to explore and go on tour
And that's me to a core.

Aaron Clark (11)
Abbeyfield School

THE ZODIAC

Do you believe in star signs,
I don't but do you?
What's your star sign if you do?
Is it Leo that lion dude?

Scorpios are pretty cool,
When's your birthday?
That's the clue,
Let everyone know at school.

Matthew Batts (13)
Abbeyfield School

LEO

The lion is the king of the jungle,
The king of animals,
The lion can growl,
The lion can roar,
The king can be sad and
The king can be mad,
The lion with his proud mane
And Leo is his name.
This is a tale of the lion.

Adam Gardner (11)
Abbeyfield School

DEVIL

The Devil tempts you.
Makes you do things you don't want to do.
With its evil glare, he makes you stare
Tempting you more and more, making you give in
To the nasty Devil with the sly grin
He fills your head with nasty things
Evilness is what he brings.
Choose the angels above.
Not the Devil, he has no love.

Louise Gandolfi (12)
Abbeyfield School

THE ZODIAC

I don't believe in zodiac,
Because it's never true,
All the fame and fortune,
It never comes to you.
The bad luck goes to everyone
And there it seems to stay.
I'm the star sign Leo
But what it says -
It never pays
Because it says I'm lucky
But I never get a penny,
So I don't believe in chance,
We make our luck in life
Zodiac pages are hardly worth a glance.

Ali Hammond (12)
Abbeyfield School

RAINDROPS

Watch the little raindrops
Running down the windowpane,
See the puddles of water,
Lying in the lane,
Hear the children playing,
Bright, shiny boots on their feet.
See the wiggly, squirmy worms,
Sliding down the street
And see the rainbow painted high
In the blue, glittering sky.

Lucy Wheeler (11)
Abbeyfield School

School

School is amazing,
School is fun,
School is the best,
But so is sucking your thumb.

School is amazing,
School is great,
School is open,
So come through the gate.

School is amazing,
School is ace,
School is excellent,
So tie up your lace.

Kirsty Steer (12)
Abbeyfield School

The Zodiac

As Pisces swims in the Milky Way
Sagittarius with powerful bow shoots outs a fiery comet
Aquarius with his golden urn scoops up a glittering galaxy,
Whilst golden Leo stands tall and proud surveying the entire universe.
Virgo in perfection sits amongst the twinkling stars,
With Gemini on the brink of sorrow yet smiling at the sun
Aries the ram is headbutting silver stars,
Cancer likes to spin the moon upon its mighty claw
Whilst Libra balances Pluto and Venus whilst
Weighing out some sun,
Scorpio teetering on its tail whilst spinning round its planet
Capricorn leaps over comets and stars and
Taurus the bull sees red and charges at an exploding burning star.

Bethany Quarmby (11)
Abbeyfield School

THE ZODIAC

Capricorn is the patient goat,
Pisces does not need a boat.
Aquarius is the water carrier,
Sagittarius is the sky warrior.
Aries is the butting ram,
Leo is not weak like a lamb.
Taurus is the charging bull,
With Gemini you're seeing double.
Cancer the crab makes a clicking sound,
Scorpio lives under rocks in the ground.
Virgo looks for love but fails,
And Libra is always balancing scales.
The zodiac includes these twelve signs,
But now it's time I ended these lines.

James Flynn (12)
Abbeyfield School

DREAMS

What will I dream?
Will I be an astronaut zooming into space,
Or will I be a funny clown with pie splattered over my face?
Or will I be a gruesome dream with wicked witches or
Will I be a horrifying monster come marching through my door?

What will I dream?
I might meet my Prince Charming who'll ride me off to see
All his gleaming treasure, what a treat it will be.
I may like life but I prefer to dream
Not nightmares but ones that are like strawberries and cream.
Short 'n' sweet.

Rebecca Watson (11)
Abbeyfield School

THE SUN AND THE MOON 'FOREVER RIVALS'

The sun in its chariot of fire,
Lies in her throne,
As the moon draws nearer,
Her flames become higher.

Golden is the horizon and scarlet is the sunset,
Misty is the eerie moon,
The clouds so high and during rainfall,
Exceedingly soaking wet.

Crimson in her fury,
The sun lay down to rest,
The sky now controlled by the moon,
Was pink and blurry.

The moon clashes with the sun,
On his silver wings,
And makes the dawn perish,
Night has begun.

The moon - his ice comforting him,
Now and always is orbiting the Earth,
His loyal rocky guardian protecting him,
From the sun - now terrifically dim.

The sun cradles her children - the stars,
Who twinkle ever so brightly,
As so do her other kids,
Including Mars.

Hannah Parker (11)
Churchfields School

THE TOWERS

The planes flew,
The planes crashed,
The towers crumbled,
The windows smashed.

The blood was shed,
The people cried,
Fifty storeys up,
They jumped and died.

They say it's bin Laden,
A cruel, cruel man,
He hides in the mountains,
Of Afghanistan.

The city stopped,
With the beat of a heart,
A tear is shed,
For loved ones apart.

They stood in silence,
Eleven was the hour,
Three minutes' remembrance,
The world has turned sour.

They say the death toll
Is thousands at least,
May all their souls
Rest in peace.

Tim Eustace (14)
Churchfields School

Who Is It?

As I sat in my favourite chair to read the local paper,
To eat my meal and pour the ground pepper;
Then all of a sudden I heard footsteps outside my chamber door.
Who it was, what it was, I was not sure.
I then looked up at the beautiful portrait of my belovéd wife,
How could God have taken her life?
The sound had stopped so I went on with my meal
I thought for a minute of crooks coming in to steal.
The noise started again but it was inside,
Then I cried,
'Who are you?'
There was silence so I resumed
I sat there rocking back in my chair,
The fear in my eyes flooding to where the noise was over there.
I thought it was my mind
But my eyes became aligned
To where stood a shadowy figure.
I thought I'd better not linger
So I went over for a look.
There was nothing there, my head automatically shook,
I sat back down
And across my forehead came a frown.
I looked at the painting, there was something different about it
Then the candle became unlit.
What was going on?
Then I heard a song.
I sat there in the dark,
There was a sharp pain in my back like I was bitten by a shark.

What happened next, no one knows
It just goes to show,
Weird things do happen.

Bethany O'Mahoney (13)
Churchfields School

JUDGEMENT DAY

I was standing on the front line,
It seemed I had just done a crime.
There comes the devils at night,
It gave us a fright.

We got out our guns,
They ran and ran.
So we thought of our mums,
And we knocked them down one by one.

The time was up,
It was all over.
More and more came,
And we did the same.

There comes the man,
The one upon the skies.
And there comes the man,
Down below the ground.

The thunder came
Knocking them down,
Their leader looked like a clown.

At last, their leader disappeared in a flash,
'Yes we won!' we all shouted.

As the dust hovered by,
We went upon the skies.
We are free at last,
We are free!

Henry Chan (12)
Churchfields School

THE SCRAMBLE

As he sat in his ramshackle deckchair,
Of the coming event he was still unaware.
Suddenly as a sharp klaxon sounded,
He jumped to his feet and to his Spitfire he bounded.
Over the loud speaker a voice came booming,
'Scramble! Godspeed! The Jerries are coming.'
He dived in the cockpit, pulled down his goggles;
He made the canopy come down with the flick of some toggles;
He rammed open the throttle, baring his teeth,
He was soon in the air, the ground disappearing beneath.
Five minutes later he could see the bandits;
The flak from the ground only gave them minor hits.
As he drew near he got a 109 in his gun sight,
He had the advantage of the sun and greater height;
He got to within 300 feet and raked it from propeller to tail.
It exploded in mid-air; the pilot had no time to bail.
His wingman had an enemy on his six,
So he turned on his wing and gave it a dose of his own tricks.
The dogfight wore on; it felt like it went on for hours,
But soon they were home, apart from Flight Lieutenant Bowers;
He'd gone down in flames, like so many men,
They'd all gone away to God's good garden.
And through the war the pilot's days were numbered;
And they shall always be remembered.

Michael Marder (12)
Churchfields School

SECRET AGENT

Driving to the location on the main road,
Breaking into the buildings by cracking the codes.
Gripping your gun, ready to pull the trigger,
In the distance there is a misty dark figure.

The trigger was pulled, the figure was dead,
He was ready to put this mission to bed.
He sped up the stairs and entered a room,
The agent had sadly reached his doom.

Stefan Mazzotta (12)
Churchfields School

Best Friends

I am so unlucky,
to have you as a friend.
You wind me up constantly,
you drive me round the bend.

My family doesn't like you,
you're loud, you smoke, you drink,
and with your bad behaviour,
sometimes you just don't think.

But other times
you're always there,
you're kind, you're helpful,
you really care.

When I need you,
you're by my side,
a better friend,
I could not find.

And so my friend,
now I see,
this friendship
is meant to be!

Rosie Timbrell (14)
Churchfields School

Basketball Player

He was on the court,
The score was naught-naught.
The minutes were ticking by,
The game was still a tie.
He had shot and missed,
The crowd still thought he was bliss.

The game was over now,
He couldn't take a bow.
He had lost the game,
He was only to blame.
He took off his vest,
He was no longer the best,
He was now worse than the rest.

He was too old to play another match,
There was no catch.
Now retired from the game,
No one now respected his name,
The humanity, humility and the shame.

Michael Deller (12)
Churchfields School

Living

Life is just one long ride,
You always die and never survive,
Whether you are rich or you are poor,
Everyone ends up at death's door,
Life is long and life is hard,
If life were a hotel it'd get no stars.

Death is freedom from your life,
Your spirit is free to do what it likes,
Your body may be decayed in the ground
But what was it really, but a cage
Keeping you down.

Vicki-Sara Chalk (14)
Churchfields School

Classical Music

Classical music . . . oh
How I hate classical music
All those people in straight black suits
And that annoying little tune played by the flutes.

With the trumpets playing so loud, so loud
And the conductor waving his big stick
Every time I hear them
I think I'm going to be sick

And then there're the drums
Oh the drums
I really can't think what to say
With them banging and crashing
And rolling and smashing
It makes me want to run away

Finally there're the violins oh no, oh no
I think I'm starting to cry
They can't play to save their lives
I want to curl up and die.

William Reynolds (14)
Churchfields School

World Cup Final

The players come out,
The cheers erupt,
The whistle blew,
The crowd stood up.

'Off,' they chanted,
The ref complied
Owen stood up,
They said 'He dived.'

Beckham runs to take the kick,
With a dummy and a little flick,
He knocks it back so accurate and sly,
Gerrard runs up and with a kick.

The ball's so swift,
It dodges the wall,
The keeper is slow,
Oh what a goal!

1-0 to England,
In Germany's face,
If it stays like this,
We can embrace.

The game was fast,
It was so dull,
It ended quick
There was no goal.

They all stood anxiously,
Waiting for the score,
Germany have lost,
And they do bore.

England have triumphed - oh, what stars,
The England team is going to go far.

Adam Webb (14)
Churchfields School

DEPRESSION

Imagine being locked in a black hole,
Alone, afraid and without a soul.
Think about being trapped and afraid,
Like you're the only person who was ever made.
Imagine the sun never comes out,
You would like to scream and shout.
Think about being unable to talk,
How painful it is to get up and walk.
Imagine a black hole swallowing you up,
Half empty not full that is the cup.
Think of what each day can bring,
Feeling, wanting, caring about nothing.
Imagine not fearing death, what could be worse
Than living your life under this horrible curse.
This is depression.

Abigail Gething (14)
Churchfields School

My Dreams

I rhyme like hell,
I have a story to tell,

You should have seen
The state I've been,

In my dreams,
I hear some screams,

All I see,
Is a mummy killer bee,

The bee comes closer to me,
Or as it seems,

And all I've been,
Is in a dream.

Kayleigh Kyson (12)
Churchfields School

School

Sometimes school is boring
In lessons I end up snoring
Sometimes school is good
I get good things in my mood

You have to try and do your best
You have to work in lessons without a rest
Some exams are really difficult
You won't try them at all

You have to try and be cool
To your friends in the school.

Tilbe Pulatmen (12)
Churchfields School

LITTLE BILLY

Little Billy full of gore
Nailed the baby to a door
Mother cried in accents faint
'Billy dear don't spoil the paint.'

Billy stood on the railway track
The engine gave a squeal
Then the engine driver got his spade
And scraped him off the wheel.

When Mother heard she cried with joy
Now her son was dead
All she needed was the baby to go
So she could spend all day in bed.

Two days later the baby died
What a mother, she never cried
She went upstairs with an aching head
And laid down in her comfy bed.

Rebecca Anscombe (12)
Churchfields School

MOTHERS

My mum is very special
On every single day,
The mum of all mums
Has her own special ways.
Every day she works real hard
Real hard to help me out.
So, I love you Mum.

David Manning (12)
Churchfields School

PRIDE OF WAR

I heard the cry of war,
And they told me my country needed me,
They offered me the Queen's shilling,
And tempted me with the kiss of a star,
So I did the only thing a hero can do,
I joined my country,
And moved to my new home of mud,
When there all I could do was fight to see my family again,
Then the days and months wore on
And I lost all sanity, and couldn't bare the noise,
Or to watch another friend die,
Amongst putrid, rotting bodies
And then the decaying carcasses turn to mere dust,
Never to be given a funeral fit for a hero
Now I lie here, blood seeping,
From all areas and I know what is to become of me
And I wondered why we go through this,
Is it for freedom?
Is it for honour?
Or is it simply for our own egos?

Claire King (15)
Churchfields School

TABLE TENNIS

Match point,
Come on I've almost won!
Just one more point,
And I'll be the champion.

My hands are shaking,
It's getting tense.
Time is short,
And the atmosphere is dense.

I've got one more serve,
He returns it in!
I'm playing well,
But I've got to win!

He hit the net,
The crowd goes wild!
I shook his hand,
And said 'Good game Dad.'

Tom Reynolds (12)
Churchfields School

WHY AM I THE LAST TO KNOW?

Why am I the last to know?
In whatever weather, rain, sun or snow
I always am the last to know

Every bit of gossip that comes out
Always seems to come to a drought
When people come to talk to me
The subject is transposed to another key

When I found out, it's only cos people shout
Loud and clear
So everybody can hear

I'm not surprised if the man on the moon
Heard before the strike of noon
When I hear it is always old
As most people have been told

I wish I was the first to know
In whatever weather, rain, sun or snow
I wish I was the first to know.

Laura Keogh (14)
Churchfields School

The Curse Of A Virgo

I have the curse of a Virgo
I fall in love too fast
And if I ever get them
It never seems to last

I have my heart broken
It never seems to mend
It goes on forever
And never seems to end

When my heart is stolen
It rips at my soul
I know I can't have them
But I can't let them go

This is a pain
A pain of the worse
Why am I a Virgo?
Why am I cursed?

Kayleigh Keville (15)
Churchfields School

Moods

As I lie in bed feeling lonely and depressed
Thinking to myself is anyone going to come
My whole body stiff and frightened
All because of one silly mood
It's not fair, my life is not worth living anymore
I'm so fed up with myself and this miserable life
Why am I so unhappy?
Sometimes I wake up hoping to die.

I pull my covers up a bit more as I daydream
About one day I would be really happy like everyone else!
The dark bedroom is making me more lonely
Or you could say upset.
What would you do with a mood like this?

Lauren Fowler (12)
Churchfields School

11TH SEPTEMBER

The 11th of September
Is never to be forgot
Loads of people died that day
Trust me I mean a lot

The plane came round the corner
At such a tremendous speed
Down came the tower
It was such a horrible deed

Some people say it was bin Laden
He lives in Afghanistan
I really really hate him
He is such an evil man

Little children died that day
Some as young as four
They had less than an hour to get out
As everyone dashed for the door

Now just a pile of rubble
Is all that remains from that day
Bin Laden is in major trouble
That's about all I can say.

Nikki Costello (12)
Churchfields School

WHERE ARE YOU?

Where are you, Mummy?
You disappeared without saying goodbye.
It was after we crashed the car,
You didn't seem very happy,
Your eyes were shut and your hands cold and numb.
Gran said you went on holiday.
Why didn't you tell me or take me?
I have always wanted to go to Spain.
Where are you, Mummy?
I cry every night and
Try to wait for your return, but
I wake up in the morning feeling lonely and cold.
Everybody at school's being nice and friendly,
Even Ashley the bully.
Where are you, Mummy?
I miss you,
Come home soon.

Natasha Taylor (12)
Churchfields School

FRIENDS

Friends have good days
Friends have bad days.
Friends have arguments
And stress each other out.
A good friend is always there for you
To talk to you if you're down.

I have arguments with my friends
But we're friends by the end of the day.
The most important thing about being a friend
Is to be there when they need you.
Stay friends as long as you live.
Just treasure them!

Becky Clements (13)
Churchfields School

Running Wild

They sound like thunder, running wild,
Father, mother and child,
They do as they like, stop when they will,
Standing up on the hills,
Coats shining, eyes bright,
Silhouetted against the light,
Intelligent and alert,
And yet covered with dirt,
Some watch and wait, tense and calm,
Making sure the rest come to no harm,
Something is hiding in the grass,
Then at last,
The lookout spies,
Two shining little eyes,
It sounds the alert and they run on,
Going, going, going, gone.

Kim Turner (14)
Churchfields School

Parents

Parents are so annoying,
they tell you what to do,
Like, don't wear too much make-up,
try to look your best,
homework must be done by six,
and always revise for tests,
don't watch too much telly,
never stay up too late,
sweets and snacks are bad for your teeth,
always tell me when you go on a girl, boy date.
so that's why parents are so annoying,
telling you what to do,
can't we make our own choices
and just be me and you!

Larissa Willimott (12)
Churchfields School

Sports

I like all kinds of sports, like
Basketball, football and games of all sorts.
If I could choose which game to play
It would be basketball any day.
I imagine myself with the ball running to the net,
All the players are after me
But they haven't caught me yet.
I finally score and the crowd start to roar,
Out of all the sports I play
The best of all is basketball.

Jamie Maynard (12)
Churchfields School

THE BIG MATCH

The players in the dressing room,
Strapping on their boots,
They all step out,
The crowd all hoot.

They come out on the pitch,
The crowd all cheer,
The captain calls them over,
They all gather near.

It starts with a hand-ball,
Going down the wing,
The striker runs a long haul,
And bangs it with a ping.

The ball hits the bar,
Unfortunate for him,
Beckham got cropped,
England's future looks dim.

Beckham is injured,
With a broken leg,
The physio comes on,
And shakes his head.

They sub him for Gerrard,
Gerrard takes the kick,
Bangs it in the top corner,
Oh what a kick.

The ref blows his whistle,
The crowd all cheer,
England have won,
Oh what a year.

Ben Smith (14)
Churchfields School

THE TRENCH

The smell and feel of war is cold,
Slaves and soldiers working in trenches,
The tragedies of many men told,
Making tombstones out of rotting old benches,

Buzzing with activity,
With airplanes overhead,
The fighting and shouting makes me plea,
For a safe house and roof over my head,

We run towards them guns a-blazing,
Many men fall on either side,
The mortar shells start the ground arising,
We retreat back with a lack of pride,

I wonder just how long it will last,
The German just the same,
We all think of our lost loves past,
We think it to be insane,

It's 1918, the fourth year gone,
The end of the war is spied,
It's too long since the last cream scone,
I wish I was one of the millions died,

The war is ended, but we don't know it,
We carry on, fighting like mad,
A bomb lands in our trench, it goes with a blast,
We're dead, with the war, I can't say I'm glad!

Andrew Smith (14)
Churchfields School

THE WRESTLING MATCH

The crowd was immense
I was standing on the stage
I looked down at my opponent
He was filled with rage

I began to walk
And climbed in the ring
I heard the noise of
Ding, ding, ding

He hits you hard
With lefts and rights
You're down on the mat
Looking up at the lights

You try to leave
But he pulls you back for more
You wish you could leave
Straight out the back door

You stumble out the ring
And pick up the belt
You look back at your opponent
But he's stumbling out

You look for your opponent
You can't find him anywhere
You've won the match
Fair and square.

Luke Stacey (12)
Churchfields School

He's Gone

I'm awake, yet I still feel like I'm dreaming.
Now I feel empty and all alone
I feel sick and my eyes hurt from crying.
One minute it's gone, one minute it's back.

Feels like only yesterday
He was only standing here with me.
My heart aches with pain
His pain has stopped, when will mine?

He's left me now and is not coming back
He's gone.

Carla Willis (12)
Churchfields School

A Different Place

Burning so hot
The walls red and smoking
How could *I* be sent to this horrible place?

I look all around, and I see someone walking.
Two little horns and a tail burning bright.
No bigger than my knee.
Its body red and glowing.
I wonder what it is?
But I really can't be sure.

Daisy Taylor (12)
Churchfields School

My Magical Box

I will put in my box,
The first ever sound of dripping water,
My dreams of the world,
The thought of having a chocolate house.

I will put in my box,
The chill down my spine from the courageous wind,
The thought of carrying an elephant on my back,
The sound of a fire engine's siren.

I will put in my box,
A blue cry from a newborn baby,
A fly's eye,
The sight of a black sun and stars.

My box will have stars and daydreams all over it,
It won't just stay one size because the whole world can fit inside,
The colour of a Caribbean island,
Bright and beautiful.

My box should travel many journeys,
One of which should be to feed the poor,
The next to a luxury beach,
Where the sun beats down on the beautiful sands.

When I say *'Goodbye,'*
When my journey is done,
My box will shut for the very last time.

Sophie Fisher (14)
Greendown Community School

My World

I will put in my world . . .

The big miaow of a cat
The cackling laugh of a hyena
The growl of the disturbed bear

In my world I will put . . .

The tip of a blade of grass
The sharp head of a pin
The tail of a dead flea

In my world I will put . . .

The trunk of an elephant
The rumble of someone's belly
The noise of pattering rain

In my world I will put . . .

A container of daisies
With a chamber of secrets
An ancient message inside

My world will be made up from . . .

A blue and green liquid
Different pieces of a jigsaw
The rays of a hot star
The leather sap of a tree

I will surf on my world and feel . . .

The chill of the wind
The heat of the sun
The spiky skin of a hedgehog
The slimy scales of a fish

In my world . . .

The Pope will be a Protestant
The Queen will live in a flat
Kids will find school fun

This is my world.

Lee Eagle (13)
Greendown Community School

My Special Box

I will put in my special box
a tiny grain of sand,
the cry of a baby,
the cold winter's air and
the summer's heat.
The yell of yellow and
the gush of green.

My box will be made of -
wishes and magic and
when you open it you will get a sudden shine from the
stars above.
All will be covered in feathers which will make it as soft as air.
It will be tied together with the gossamer of a spider's web
and will smell of the scented sea whirling in a spiral.

I would send it on a journey through the air
until it landed
somewhere where children can appreciate
the contents and then add to the box.

Laura Brown (13)
Greendown Community School

My Magic Box

In my box I will have . . .
The swishing of the salty sea gliding slowly over the serene sand
So smooth and elegant
The miraculous, mysterious movement of the moon
Circling the Earth every second
The silky petals of a flower
So soft and small
The heavy thud of an enormous elephant
So forceful that the ground shakes
The peaceful flight of a butterfly
Barely audible
The tiny tip of an eyelash
So miniature that it is hardly visible
The taste of a thousand grains of salt falling upon my tongue
Very sour and sweet
The whistle of the wind whirling around the leaves
On a cold winter's day

My box is manufactured by the magical hands of a carpenter
Shiny metal on the outside with decorative indentations
Very hard and durable
Foam in the middle to soften the look, with purple silk surrounding it

My box, full with my surprises, will travel to the exciting,
adventurous child's heaven
A theme park
With the loud laugh of screaming children
Roaring like thunder as they go from ride to ride
And the anxious movements of the visitors
Dashing around to buy drinks and ice creams
Just imagine . . .

Kaylie Hill (13)
Greendown Community School

My Magical Box

My magical box
What's inside?
Let's see the secrets my box can hide.
I turn the key made from pure gold
My box's secrets about to unfold.
So in I put a tiger's tail, a sharp silent scream,
And the shell of a snail.
Sharp broken silence, a tough tree trunk, the edge of an ear
And the smell of a skunk . . .
I put in my box
The claws of a cat walking on a path,
The splosh of the soap as it falls in my bath.
A high pitched scream from a bird or an ape
The rattle of bars as it tries to escape.
Heat from a fire, the coldness of ice,
The heaviness of a tyre and the tang of spice.
I put in my box
A light blue whisper from across the sea
Someone screaming or calling at me.
Inside I put night and day and a distant star that's fading away.
I put in my box
A moon shining purple, a fly on its back
All the colours in the universe from pure white to black.
I fill it with thoughts from deep in my head
And the softness of sheets that lie on my bed.
Last but not least, I fill it with fear
Followed shortly after with a fresh fallen tear.
On the outside I leave it simple and plain
Then I walk away wondering when it will be opening again.

Joanne Garrett (13)
Greendown Community School

In My Box I Would Put . . .

In my box I would put:
the sound of laughing children, playing in the street,

The soft touch of a bird's feather
drifting slowly down in windy weather,

In my box I would put:
the strange scene of the sun setting in the morning.

In my box you could step in and feel the sizzling surface of the sun,
burning like a fiery coal in a furnace,

My box would be fashioned from icing, glistening and delicate.
Metal, smooth and shiny, stars from the galaxy, sharp and sparkling,

My box will be held together with a wooden lock and key,
twinkling with the glint of pearls from the depths of the sea,

In my box you would see the first and last things on our planet,
a baby's hand and a speck of golden sand,

In my box you could experience the outside of a particle of ice,
glistening and shining,
the inside, white and refreshing.

My box would journey down through the Earth and up into space
in a time capsule embarking on a frantic race.

Abbie Cooke (13)
Greendown Community School

The Whistle

As I lie in the cold damp trench
Waiting for the whistle to blow
I watch the clouds in the blood-red sky
A rush of wind sends shivers up my spine

The whistle's blown
Over the top
The stampede of soldiers
Like stallions
Their boots thudding against the ground

The screech of rifles
Then the reply of machine guns
The screams of men
A rush of blood throughout my body

Wounded fall as if death touched them
With his icy cold fingers.

Then . . . an enormous silence.

Martyn Dearing (13)
Greendown Community School

Kitten

Winter - tiny kitten curled up sleeping by the fire,
Purring to its heart's desire.
Spring - playful kitten chasing shadows,
Soon she'll be exploring meadows.
Summer - stretched out lying in the shade,
Passing birds will be afraid.
Autumn - furry kitten sneaking around,
To pounce on leaves upon the ground.

Pippa Wright (11)
Lavington Comprehensive School

SPACE

Space is dark
Space has jagged edges
Space has no friends
Once you are in you can't escape

Space is fun
You can float in it
Fly to the stars and back
Space needs us

Earth is dark
Earth is full of war
Earth has lots of bad people
Earth's only friend is the moon

Earth is round and bubbly
Earth has lots of people living on it
Earth has control over its people
Earth has peace between its many different humans.

Jack Walker (11)
Lavington Comprehensive School

MONKEY BUSINESS

Cheeky monkey hanging around,
Sneaky monkey not making a sound.
Hairy monkey combing his hair,
Silly monkey going nowhere.
Baby monkey sucking his thumb,
Daddy monkey saying well done.
All the monkeys having fun,
All except one who's still sucking his thumb.

Celyn Spear (11)
Lavington Comprehensive School

ROLLER COASTER

The roller coaster has begun,
Slowly higher towards the sun,
At the top it gradually moves,
Towards the drop, the carriage in twos,
Suddenly it shoots down,
Also spinning round and round,
Up, down, loop the loop,
Now it goes into a hoop,
This roller coaster is so fast,
How long is it going to last,
Now down a 100 foot drop,
Round the corner and stop,
The roller coaster has come to an end,
I'm off to go on it again.

Jack Haigh (11)
Lavington Comprehensive School

FELINE FRIEND

My feline friend is happy
I wouldn't sell him to another chappy
My feline friend waits to pounce
But doesn't weigh an ounce
My feline friend doesn't hiss
And gives me a big old kiss
My feline friend is really clever
And licks me when I am under the weather
My feline friend arches her back
My poem has ended and my name is Jack.

Jack Pike (11)
Lavington Comprehensive School

The Duel

The sheriff stood and glanced at his watch,
He lifted his glass and downed his scotch.
Looking around him he saw on the wall,
The meanest animals of them all.
On the wanted poster was a portrait,
Of Big Bad Billy and his villainous mate.
As he stood leant against the bar,
The saloon doors were swung afar.
There Billy stood, blocking the light,
Holsters unclipped, ready to fight!
The sheriff cried, 'What's this about?'
Big Bad Billy said, 'I'm calling you out!'
In a couple of seconds they were stood back to back,
The undertaker watching, dressed all in black.
They took their ten paces, then they turned,
The bullets shot out, the gunpowder burned!
With one clean shot straight to the head,
An onlooker screamed, 'Bad Billy is dead!'

Jamie Grace (13)
Lavington Comprehensive School

Christmas

I like the smell of Christmas
Mince pies and Christmas pud
If I could have it every day
I definitely would

The lights upon the Christmas tree
The presents underneath
Looking out for holly
To make Mum's Christmas wreath

On Christmas Eve when we go to bed
And Santa's in his slay
He rushes round to everyone
For the start of Christmas Day.

Hugo Manning (11)
Lavington Comprehensive School

FAIRIES IN THE WOOD

At the bottom of my great gran's garden
The mystic woods of Wales lie,
I take one step, then two
Because something catches my eye
I find myself walking further into the woods
Then suddenly out pops Red Riding Hood.
I look ahead and what do I see?
All the fairytale characters, dancing with glee

Suddenly I started to feel light and airy,
I realised I was flying with a fairy
We flew over a giant fair and saw
Elves laughing, dragons dancing, pixies playing
And unicorns prancing
Then the fairy took me to a small tent in the corner
She led me in and then went straight out

A mystical woman was sitting at a small wooden table
She clapped her hands one, two, three
And I woke up very suddenly
I was in my gran's bedroom I looked out of her window
And there was a flash of light
That caught my eye mysteriously on the warm summer's night.

Sarah Evans (11)
Lavington Comprehensive School

PUPPIES

Puppies playing
Puppies barking
Yelping when left alone
Puppies sleeping, puppies eating
Happy when you're playing

Puppies biting
Puppies ripping
Acting innocent when around
Puppies naughty, puppies naughty
Playing, biting, crying
Puppies playing, puppies barking, puppies biting

Puppies sleeping
Beds
Sofas
By the fire

Puppies biting
Cushions
Toys
Wooden beds

Puppies playing
Teddies
People
Squeaky toys

Puppies ripping
Pillows
Clothes
Cotton sofas

Puppies naughty
Puppies chewing
Puppies playing
What a puppy if it doesn't!

Becky Degville (11)
Lavington Comprehensive School

As Autumn Falls

Grey, fluffy clouds slowly drifting past the moon,
Everyone can tell that cold snow's coming soon,
Terrifying, darkness engulfs the bright sky,
Frightens the poor animals as they scurry by.

The haunting sound of wind brushing past the trees,
Making you shiver from your spine to your knees,
The distant sound of wolves howling in the light,
Daunting, eerie, echoing sounds in the night.

Sense the coldness of the occasional dew,
As it gently falls down and soaks into you,
Chilling sounds of rain as it drips to the ground,
Goosebumps occur as you listen to the sound.

Random creaks, scrapes and groans of ancient branches,
As stunning landscapes transfix you in trances,
Trees swaying in the everlasting gales,
Unearthing shrubs with strength like forest snails.

The cold gets heavier as night progresses,
The animals sleep, hidden in the hedges,
Shadows flickering against the forest walls,
The last leaf of autumn gently sways, then falls.

Samantha Page (11)
Lavington Comprehensive School

GUESS WHO?

You!
Your feet are as strong as a building.
You!
Your tail is as long as a tape measure.
You!
Your claws are as sharp as razor blades.
You!
Your fur is as golden as the sun.
You!
Your whiskers are as sensitive as landmines.
You!
Your teeth are like prongs stabbing into you.
You!
Your eyes are as precise as a rifle aim.
You!
Your roar is as loud as an Earth-shattering avalanche.

Nicholas Rollinson (12)
Lavington Comprehensive School

MY ANIMAL POEM

Your roar is like a fire bell that has been hit with a hammer
Your pounce is like a gentle trickling waterfall
Your family is called the cat family
Your tail is like a striped giraffe neck
Your teeth are like sharp knives
Your fur is like a fake fur rug
Your eyes are like binoculars
Your nose is like a pink heart
Your claws are like pins.

Hannah Light (11)
Lavington Comprehensive School

My Animal Poem

You
Your claws are as sharp as broken glass
You
Your tail is as long as a giraffe's neck
You
Your fur is as hairy as a chimpanzee
You
Your colour is as colourful as a crayon
You
Your eyes are as small as my pencil lead
You
Your whiskers are as parallel as the Empire State Building
You
Your ears are as spiky as the end of a Concorde.

Michael Henderson (12)
Lavington Comprehensive School

The Future

On a planet in years to come,
Where people play and have fun,
No more buses, cars or taxis
To harm our skies or threaten our lungs.
Where spaceships fly around the skies
Ferrying the people around,
Robots taking over our menial tasks
Glad to be useful at last.
Promises hold our future gaze
As a planet we can fulfil our dreams
No more bombs and no more wars
A place of harmony among the races.

Harry Rice (12)
Lavington Comprehensive School

THE CUDDLIEST DOG

You
Your fur is as smooth as a piece of silk.
You
Your legs are as long as table legs.
You
Your tail is as soft as a pillow.
You
Your nose is as cold as an iceberg.
You
Your mouth is as nice as a puppy.
You
Your eyes are as nice as a baby's face.
You
Your claws are as sharp as a blade.
You
Your whiskers are as nice as a monkey just been born.
You
Your ears are smoother than a feather.
You
Your colour is as beautiful as a butterfly.

Ashley Buck (11)
Lavington Comprehensive School

GUESS MY THING!

You
Your ears are as pointy as freshly sharpened pencils
You
Your eyes glow like two car headlights.
You
Your tail is as wiggly as fine rubber.
You
Your tongue is as rough as sandpaper.

You
Your whiskers are as long as tails.
You
Your colour is as black and white as a blackboard with chalk.
You
Your purr is as roaring as a car engine.
You
Your back is as arched as a bridge.

Charlotte Cox (11)
Lavington Comprehensive School

THE SPRINGY MONKEY

You!
Your voice is like a jet.
You!
Your mouth is as wide as the world.
You!
Your legs are as bouncy as springs.
You!
Your arms are as long as the universe.
You!
Your eyes are as brown as chocolate.
You!
Your tail is like a curly snake.
You!
Your fur is as wiry as wires.
You!
Your colour is as brown as chairs.
You!
Your feet are like cheese.

Jade Eva (11)
Lavington Comprehensive School

MYSTERY CAT

I always think I'd like to be,
a mysterious pussycat,
prowling along the rooftops high
and lying on the mat.

I'd like to pounce on little mice
and chase them all away
and climb upon my scratching pole
and enjoy a peaceful day.

They always look so cunning,
as they curl up on the rug
and sit there purring peacefully,
ready for a hug.

How I would like to climb and hiss
and prowl around at night,
but no, not I, can do those things,
my eyes must be shut tight.

Oh how I have to go to school
and learn my ABC,
if only I were a cat,
I would be tickled constantly.

Jade Shields (11)
Lavington Comprehensive School

MONKEY

Your voice is like the horn of a car
You
Your lips are like a rubber fan belt
You
Your legs are as bendy as a cheese string
You

Your arms are as strong as a crowbar
You
Your eyes are as round as the sun
You
Your tail is as long as a metre stick
You.

Wayne Bedwell (11)
Lavington Comprehensive School

You

You
Your fur is as soft as a pillow.
You
Your teeth are as sharp as needles.
You
Your claws are as long as a pole.
You
Your tail is as long as a chair.
You
Your eyes are as round as the sun.
You
Your colour is as patchy as a cow.
You
Your feet are as big as your body.
You
Your tummy is as round as a barrel.
You
Your tongue is as long and wet as a flannel.
You
Your ears are as floppy as tissue paper.
You
Your nose is as soggy and round as a button.

Harriet Lacey (11)
Lavington Comprehensive School

MERCURY

I was dozing in my bed one night,
Looking at the stars so bright,
Thinking of what it would be like,
To live up on Mercury.

Is it joyful or is it bad
Or is it a place that drives you mad?
Are there monsters or naughty ghosts
That come on a Sunday and nick all the roasts?

Is there war and is there pain
Or are there no people on this terrain?
Is it lonely and is it dark
Or is it like children playing in the park?

I want to go up to that planet
To see if anyone lives in granite.
What sort of things do they eat
And do they bury people in mud or in peat?

Is there brightness like beautiful flowers?
Are there bridges and huge towers?
Are there holidays and places to go?
Well I gather in my life I'll never know.

Craig Campbell (12)
Lavington Comprehensive School

CAT POEM

His name is Patch,
He has a fabulous catch,
Every night he goes out on hunts,
Sometimes using marvellous stunts,
He'll leap, he'll sleep, your company he'll keep.

Every night he goes out on the prowl,
If he meets other cats he'll scowl,
He'll always hiss,
But mainly kiss
He'll leap, he'll sleep, your company he'll keep.

Lydia Degville (11)
Lavington Comprehensive School

It . . .

It's with you in the summer breeze
It's with you up the mountain
It's with you when your mother dies
It's with you when you cry.

It's such a strange and twisted word
You don't know what it means
You see it flying high up there
It slips just out of reach.

It's up there with the planets
Floating around in space
It's down there with the heavens
Fearing a moment's grace.

It's there with your money
It's there with your success
It's there with your future
It's there with your rest.

It's there when you move
It's in a different world
It's about with the strangers
It's complete now it's told.

Sarah Woods (13)
Lavington Comprehensive School

ME

Me
My eyes are as green as paint
Me
My nails are as short as freshly cut grass
Me
My teeth are as white as snow
Me
My legs are as long as ladders
Me
My feet are as smelly as cheese
Me
My cheeks are as rosy as apples
Me
My hair is as brown as chocolate.

Hannah Collins (11)
Lavington Comprehensive School

IN THE MIDDLE OF THE NIGHT

In the middle of the night,
When it's very, very late,
And even dogs are dreaming,
Outside the air is cold and still,
And the frost is glinting and gleaming.

In the middle of the night,
When the moon is bright and stark,
And the trees stand bare and haggard,
Against the dark night sky,
The houses look deserted and ragged.

In the very early morning,
When another day has dawned,
And the village awakens once more,
The chill of winter begins to fade,
And the ground gets ready to thaw.

Laura Podger (12)
Lavington Comprehensive School

PEGASUS

Mounting the silvery, velvet steed,
The power below overwhelms,
Rising up, flying high above trees, the world,
Galloping through mares' tails,
Beneath the restful beat of white feathered wings,
Rise and fall,
Snuggling into the warmth of the fleecy white coat.
Gaining speed, getting faster and faster,
Bubbling with excitement,
Your heart is soaring higher than the moon,
Fringed with fear,
Wind whipping your face as you go through icy air.

Gradually slowing to a steady, rhythmical beat,
Slow as a feather drifting to the floor.
Silky mane and tail flying behind,
Fingers gripping the flowing mane,
Ears that prick forward through cool, gentle breezes
And gushing winds,
Battling storms, skimming swiftly along fresh winds,
Flying high into oblivion.

Becky Smallman (11)
Lavington Comprehensive School

Snake Alert

In hot, hot Africa lives the snake,
It slithers, silently through the long grass,
Searching to find some prey.
Its huge mouth, waters with hunger,
Or is it just venom waiting to kill?
It searches for hours on end,
But, as the sun goes down
The snake catches sight of a
Desert rat!
The snake rushes over quickly,
Poison fills its mouth
And crunch,
The rat's dead!
This was a good meal.
Satisfied, the snake slithers off into the sunset.

Mike Dagnall (11)
Lavington Comprehensive School

Writing Poetry

My favourite place is somewhere secret,
somewhere nobody knows where I am,
I sit there thinking about what lies ahead,
And I always discuss it with Sam.

I sit and I think, and I drink and I wink,
At my best friend forever called Sam,
I think to myself what a wonderful place,
And how wonderfully lucky I am.

I think about hobbies and pets, and school
And my other favourite places,
Like under the stairs, where nobody cares,
And under a tree, where all I know is me.

So here I am in my favourite place,
All alone . . . just me,
And I sit and I think and I drink and I wink,
At my best friend sat under the tree.

Katherine Sawyer (13)
Lavington Comprehensive School

THE SIMILE CAT

You!
Your claws are as long as a tape measure.
You!
Your tail is big as a fence post.
You!
Your fur is as hairy as a bush.
You!
Your colour is like a wooden fence.
You!
Your eyes are as dark as a dark street.
You!
Your whiskers are as long as the Empire State Building.
You!
Your ears are as big as a train tunnel.

John Neale (11)
Lavington Comprehensive School

WHERE TO SLEEP

Our cat
Sleeps anywhere
On the table
On the chair.
With the washing
On my bed
Cuddling up to
Erin's ted.
On the floor
By the door
He doesn't care
Our cat sleeps
Anywhere.

Jack Meech (11)
Lavington Comprehensive School

WHALE POEM

I'm a little whale, 1, 2, 3
I swim all day throughout the sea
I love to dive and splash about
And sometimes I like to sing and shout!
But when I get hungry I swim right down
To the seabed and shuffle around
For my small snack you cannot see
So I guess it should be all for me
The only thing I hate to see, is the killing of the ones
Just like me.

Tom Cassin-Davies (12)
Lavington Comprehensive School

Cats

A sleek, black creature,
With a nimble feature.
Squeeze him too tightly he'll hiss and spit,
Be kind and gentle he'll be a playful kit.
He'll pounce at his prey,
Nothing will make him stay.
Miaow, miaow, miaow!

A greedy cat,
Always fat.
Lazily purring away,
Never ever gets up to play.
Deep in thought,
Nothing will be caught.
Purr, purr, purr!

As cunning as a fox,
Though slyer than a box.
Slinking into shadows,
Arching its back at baddows.
Staring at the night,
A mysterious sight.
Prowling, prowling, prowling!

As brave as a lion,
As shiny as a diamon'.
More clever than a detective,
Very protective.
Leaps to find,
A good place to climb.
Leaping, leaping, leaping.

A sleek, black creature!

Holly John (11)
Lavington Comprehensive School

The Creature Of The West

The creature of the west,
Do you know what I'm on about
Because if you don't you'll soon find out
Let me tell whilst you create.

I've seen the creature soaring in the sunset
As it hurries to its land,
I've heard its haunting scream
In the darkness to give us all a spook goodnight.

Its scaly skin no longer rough
For now it's as smooth as silk
And as for its shine
It glistens, like a crystal chandelier.

Its land I will see
But for now
I will only study the beast
'Cause I'm the only one who has seen

Sometime I'll catch this magical beast
Somehow in this beast's land,
Maybe there will be more
In this world of wisdom beyond.

I will leave you
To make up this magical creature
And to imagine and use your spirit
To turn it into what I've seen.

Danielle Freeman (11)
Lavington Comprehensive School

The Street Child

The weather is near freezing,
The wind is whistling by,
A street child lies in a doorway,
And no one hears it sigh.

The snow, it falls in thick flakes,
The lake has frozen over,
The street child sits in the ice and cold,
The fields have lost their clover.

His mother has abandoned him,
His sister died in sleep,
His father left him at his birth,
And now he sleeps in sleet.

Christmas time is nearing,
Last minute shoppers hurry by,
All too wound up in their lives,
No one hears a small child's cry.

Christmas time is over,
And the street child now is dead,
He lies, unnoticed, near a road,
With snow used as his bed.

This ending should be different,
But through the fault of you and I,
That freezing, unloved, innocent child,
Lay in the snow to die.

Samantha Birch (13)
Lavington Comprehensive School

THE ALIEN

Spaceships away we go,
Go, go, go just keep the flow,
Antennas, rockets,
To the moon,
Hope to see you very soon.

Flashing lights,
Throughout the night,
Space, rockets,
Jupiter, Mars,
Hope to see you in your buggy cars.

Fly, fly, fly on by,
Making noises in the sky,
Stars, planets,
Neptune, Saturn,
Hope to see you pass the baton.

Whizz, whoosh,
Swish, swoosh,
Mercury, Venus
And the sun,
I'll be back when my job's done.

Stacey Fielding (11)
Lavington Comprehensive School

JELLYFISH

Squid helps for big feast
Jellyfish all gather here
Angelfish swim far

Shark joins, eats up food
Jellyfish stings him on the nose
Piranhas bite humans

Sharks miss out on food
Jellyfish get full on food
The feast is over

Jellyfish go to bed
Sharks come back and eat them up
They've had their feast.

Dominic Walmsley (12)
Lavington Comprehensive School

THE SEA

The sea is a casket of dreams waiting to be unlocked.
Colours emerge into shapes of magical mystery.
Unthinkable thoughts drift through minds that time has forgotten.
Creatures sing a song of love, beauty and knowledge.
Unknown mysteries hidden in the depths of glistening blue water.
Time stops while outside life goes on in the upper world.
Plant life waltzes with the waves on ocean floors.
The sound of the sea calms the wildest souls.
Peace is with the Earth while the ocean is listening.
The balance treasured by past and present generations.
Sapphire waves show their majesty to the skies.
Life is serene in the jewel that is the sea.

Emma L Hancock (12)
Lavington Comprehensive School

FOOTBALL'S COMIN' HOME

Football is great
Football is fun
Football keeps you on the run.

Cheers from the crowd
Cheers from the fans
Cheers from the people in the TV vans

First comes the yellow
Then comes the red
And then comes an early bath and quick get to bed

There's no need to whinge
There's no need to whine
It's your own fault you got the fine

You're not allowed to play for a couple of matches
You get suspended
Just because you get the red

You're allowed to play again
You prove yourself
By going round one and another

You're on an amazing run
You're finally at the edge of the box
You see your chance
And take a shot

The goalie's fooled by the curl
It's off the post
You're in for the rebound
You do a scissors kick

Goal Lazio!
Your manager gives you
A pay rise
You're back in business.

Ben McGowan (11)
Lavington Comprehensive School

Ode To An Old Steam Engine

In its working life
It was used for sawing wood and threshing corn
Then they left it in a field
Laying rusting and forlorn

Rust was silently eating away
At the front right wheel's rim
The canopy supports were rotten
Making the canopy cave in

The piston was truly seized
Into the cylinder block
But a good hard tap from a hammer
Could make it come unstuck

But then it was discovered
By an enthusiast who had heard the story
That the engine could be restored
To its original former glory.

A new front right wheel
And the engine was painted green
Then a new canopy
Now the engine's a common sight
On the rally scene.

Christopher Perkins (11)
Lavington Comprehensive School

I Saw A Pony

I saw a pony running wild
And alongside her was her child,
A beautiful mare galloping by,
Of black and brown with a shine in her eye.
Her little foal with tiny hooves,
The way they walk and trot and move,
Makes my heart jump out of my chest,
I want to stroke them when they rest.
I want to have them, they look so fine,
Oh how I wish they were mine,
No bridle, saddle not a bit,
Or any other riding kit.
They're free to go wherever they wish,
Like a bird in the air or a sea of swimming fish
And over the horizon several shapes did appear,
They were graceful and elegant, I needed not fear.
They cantered up closer I suddenly knew,
That these shapes were horses and ponies that flew.
The beautiful mare galloped away,
Her foal close behind, oh I wish they would stay,
The herd was reunited once more,
They trotted away, dust rose from the floor,
Then when it settled there wasn't a trace,
That a herd of ponies were here, in this very place
And after that I never saw them again,
I only remember her silky black mane.
But I do sometimes see them inside of my mind,
Just strutting around oh so gentle and kind,
I'll see them again, but when I don't know
I follow my heart or the path of a crow.

Katy Bristow (11)
Lavington Comprehensive School

THE QUEEN CAT

There she lies,
Dressed in a luxurious robe of mottled fur,
Walk shy silken paws
And a continuously whispering purr

But going beyond that peaceful look
Searching further than that world of ours . . .

A land of dreams and awesome powers
Where a single day lasts a hundred hours

She sits on a throne of tasselled pillows
Carried in a sedan chair
Stroking her fur as she goes
With a feline pedicure on fingers and toes.

As she brushes away the hanging vines
A scene is revealed like never before
An orchard of bushes, twisted and queer
Their colours amazing, opalescent and sheer

Surrounding this mass of fabulous plants
Were cats that one cannot compare
Carrying punnets full to the brim
With cream, catnip, lace and trim
Gadgets and gizmos and pussy-like things
All for her, these offerings

Suddenly one emerald eye
Leisurely opens, but with disappointment
As she realises the world is not quite like her dreams
Of thrones and of catnip floating down streams.

Lauren Sankey (11)
Lavington Comprehensive School

GONE SHOPPING

Get in the car, turn the engine on,
Step on the pedal and we're gone.
Where's a parking space, I can't fit in that,
This silly car is far too fat.
Are you going mate,
Cos I'm running late.
Finally I've found a space,
Come on Martin do up your lace.
Our shopping list is:
Beans, greens,
Rice, ice,
Cheese, peas,
Coffee, toffee,
Party popper, bottle topper
And that'll do.
Martin you get beans, greens, rice, ice and cheese,
I'll get party popper, bottle stopper, coffee, toffee, peas.
Now to the till,
It's going to be a big bill.
Bag it up,
Put it in the boot.
Get in the car, turn the engine on,
Step on the pedal and we're gone.

Sam Hayward (12)
Lavington Comprehensive School

BOY'S BEST FRIEND

Comically chases squirrels,
She can't climb trees,
She digs holes and more holes,
The best foot warmer on a cold night.

She always listens,
She's totally trusting,
The best secret keeper,
Her all knowing brown eyes let me know
She's my best friend.

Michael Askey (11)
Lavington Comprehensive School

Christmas Time

Christmas is here again
Happy faces and relations here
I can't wait for Christmas Day
I can't wait, filled up stocking right to the full
Christmas Eve is so exciting
When Santa is riding all night
To find all the children on Christmas Day.

All the presents,
You wake up at six o'clock in the morning
All excited
All the food now getting ready
The turkey smelling fabulous
Christmas pudding flavoured in brandy
And Christmas pudding is smelling of the brandy
Poured for the fire for enjoyment

Everyone is sitting round the table ready for the food
People eating the fabulous food
Everyone having a brilliant time
Then you get to open your presents from all the family
And have even more fun now your parents go to sleep
Because they are so tired
From all the work they have been doing.

Toby Mullins (11)
Lavington Comprehensive School

My Dog Monty

When you were young I came to call
To meet you, a fluffy little ball
The fattest pup with ears of silk
First to get at your mum's milk

Then you came home to us in Tilted
We bought you a lead and gave you a bed
And you were fun, never a bore
You left your message on the floor

So yes you were a naughty pup
You always chewed our slippers up
You scratched at doors and jumped up trees
And bought us presents like your fleas

When people come they ring the bell
And if you're there you give them hell
You have got a really scary bark
And sometimes you leave a mark

When you trapped your tail in the door
It left a mark and it was sore
And your black, wet nose
Well it tickles my toes

Your paws are really rough
And your teeth are extremely tough
Your breath is like cheese
It comes out a smelly breeze

My mum likes to take you on walks
And when you come back your fur's full of stalks
You love to jump into pools full of mud
They stop you panting and cool down your blood

And so I am sure you will always love me
Like I love you my darling Monty.

Kerry Lacey (11)
Lavington Comprehensive School

The Ultimate Try

Johnny was on the wing
Waiting for the ball
The forwards packed in a scrum
Ready for the call

The crowd began to sing
As Johnny stamped the ground
The rain beat down like a drum
The forwards wheeled around

The scrum half passed it out
And it was passed out
Along the backs to Johnny's hands
And in his mind he had no doubt

To score to win the cup
Johnny dodged two men and two more
Before the rest could spoil his plans
He crossed the line to score.

Rory Davis (12)
Lavington Comprehensive School

A Football Ballad

It was Sunday morning,
the day was boring
but it was football Sunday,
ten o'clock and I was gone.

We were off to Swindon,
against Swindon Town Rangers,
but we are the Power Rangers,
there were still a lot of strangers.

The keeper took the kick,
our player got the ball,
he didn't know which player to pick,
he passed the ball, he lobbed the keeper, goal.

Half-time the whistle goes,
we have a drink,
the wind blows,
oh no, they get a goal!

I got tackled, so much pain,
the ref came and said free kick,
my pain caused some rain,
the match was cancelled, oh no!

I was going home to see my mum,
but I'd had a lot of fun,
I asked my mum, 'What could I do?'
she replied 'I do not know.'

The day was over
and I was bored
so I was mad and I roared
but I calmed down and went to bed.

Robert Williams (12)
Lavington Comprehensive School

The Damage Boy

He destroys everything that he has
He destroys everything his parents own
He rips the wallpaper off the wall
He tears the wallpaper in the hall.

He loves his parents
He hates them too
But he loves them more
Even to the centre core.

He punctures the pipes in the loo
By using a metal, solid screw
He turns the taps fully round
He squirts bleach on the ground.

He makes his mum cry all the time
Because of what he does
He kills the fish in the tank
And he makes the water mank.

He cuts the mattress day and night
Even if it's in the light
He runs his mum up the wall
He makes her run round the hall.

He scratches the table
He cuts the cable
He cuts the sofa
And he breaks the fridge.

He breaks the plants
He scratches the car
He ruins the house
And he killed his mouse.

James Wall (12)
Lavington Comprehensive School

Why Did It Have To Happen?

Grandad I love you.

Why did you have to die,
Way before my time,
Why did you have to go away,
Thoughts of you are always mine.

Where did you go,
Oh grandad of mine,
Why wasn't there enough of
Life's time?

I wish you could have,
Been here now,
To watch me grow,
I wonder how.

I wish you could have,
Held me tight
And given me a little kiss
And said goodnight.

Monday is your birthday,
The 1st of October
And if you were here,
I'd invite you over.

My stepdad would have
Liked to have met you,
Kirsty your new granddaughter,
Sure would have too.

I'll love you forever,
More than I can say,
I miss you more
And more every day.

Grandad I love you.

Hannah Emm (13)
Lavington Comprehensive School

My Dog

My dog's got a strange attitude,
It's more than complicated.
Sometimes he's lively, sometimes not,
Always acting as if he's hungry.

Every day he'll have a funny five minutes,
He'll race round the garden
At a million miles an hour,
Eating heads off flowers.

He could eat for England,
There's only one food he hates.
Tomatoes, he hates tomatoes,
They're his nightmare.

He always likes to have a nap,
He's too big to sleep on your lap.
Although he is aware of this,
He really doesn't care.

He's black and shiny,
Barky and whiny,
With a waggly tail,
Ears that flop about.

Lucy MacDonald (12)
Lavington Comprehensive School

AUTUMN

Sunlight streaming through the ravaged trees,
Wind whispering past fallen leaves.
Leaves that are turning golden and red,
Scraping branches that lean overhead.
A field of corn flowing with the breeze,
The farmer's tool lashing with ease.
Swallows glide to a faraway place,
To escape that frozen winter face.
Squirrels and hedgehogs scurry away,
To store more food for that first winter's day.
Autumn, the season of so many colours,
Purples, reds, yellows and others.
The last leaf settles slowly on the ground,
The trees are bare, mist swirls around.
The sun beams pale and golden rays,
Slowly weakening as the Earth rotates.
Through all its seasons, balancing forever,
Endlessly, relentlessly, ceasing never.

Rachael Vaughan (13)
Lavington Comprehensive School

WAR

War is when someone hates someone else,
For personal vendetta or for their beliefs,
But war happens between countries,
This can affect many hundreds of innocent people.

War is endless with countless lives being lost,
With no winners,
Just losers.

War is hatred,
The opposite to love,
And if love was everywhere,
Then we could work together to live better lives.

Steven Hatton-Pocklington (14)
Lavington Comprehensive School

THE FORGOTTEN PONY

The forgotten pony,
lay out on the moor,
cold and crisp.
He's so lonely.

Fur overgrown,
from being out on
the moor for so long.
Always alone.

The Shetland strayed to the moor,
when his master died,
he returned every day
and called.

Only one person knew
a lady who strolled
over the rocky moor
forever in blue.

He became attached to
this lady and drew closer
and closer day by day
to the lady in blue.

The forgotten pony,
now had a home.
Not anymore,
is he lonesome.

There is not a forgotten pony,
who lays out on the moor,
cold and crisp.
He's not lonely.

Laura Kyte (12)
Lavington Comprehensive School

ONE NIGHT

One gloomy, scary night,
When the stars were glowing,
I was in my warm bed,
With formidable thoughts in my head.

I was in a dark room,
When I heard an almighty boom,
Should I go and have a peek
Or should I stay put and not speak?

I went to have a little look
And I saw a giant book,
I opened it up
And blue and white ghosts shot up.

I woke in my warm, stuffy bed,
With an enormous wallop on my head,
I got out of bed,
With the bump on my head,

I went down the stairs
And I saw my mum, Claire,
'I heard a loud noise last night,
Were you alright?'

I had a bad dream,
I could almost scream.

Charlie Cook (12)
Lavington Comprehensive School

FOOTBALL CRAZY

The tension mounts
The crowd take their seats
The players come out
In their colourful kits
The whistle blows
The ball gets moving
He is not offside

Goal
Lazio
The crowd cheers
The manager goes mental
The players do a crazy celebration
The goalkeeper puts his face in his hands
The losing team get sadly on their bus
This is the start of a night of busy pubs

Dawn breaks
Over a happy nation
It's a world record of the amount of people with a hangover
They will be okay in a week or so for the next game
That's all we have time for tonight so from John and me
Goodnight
PS - cut down on the beers
And don't forget to tune in next week on BBC1.

Luke Pullen (11)
Lavington Comprehensive School

Sweet Dreams

Trees made from lollies,
Icing on the moon,
All the gingerbread people,
Know that winter's coming soon.

Houses made of shortbread,
Fields of candyfloss,
Growing on chocolate logs,
Sherbet as the moss.

Frosting on the streams,
Snow is nearly here,
All the gingerbread people,
Know that winter is near.

Trees are going hard,
Birds are flying south,
People are gathering sweets and nuts
And putting them in their mouths.

Gates of chocolate disappear,
Now all the gingerbread people,
Know that winter is here.

Everything is fast asleep,
The coconut snow falls down in a heap,
Yet the Jelly Tot bushes are still in bloom,
The place in the sky.

I paddle my feet in a lemonade stream,
Then wake up with a jolt
It's just a *sweet dream.*

Kelly Corson (12)
Lavington Comprehensive School

LIFE AND LAZINESS

It started out as a normal day,
everything was going my way.
I got up, out and started yawning,
it looked like it was late in the morning.

I crawled out of bed and in my room,
all I could see was daylight.
I went to see my dog in his box,
because last night he barked at a fox.

I got dressed and had some lunch
and said, 'I love my life.'
I went down to make a roll,
and cut it with a kitchen knife.

I put on a CD and jumped around,
I was bored and put on a video.
I lazed around until time for dinner
and then made up a song called 'The Sinner'.

I proceeded ready for bed
and looked at the stars,
it looked like I could see Mars.

I buried in bed and was drifting off,
then I woke to hear a bark,
but it was still late and sunless.

I fell back to sleep until it was day
and finally I had my way.

Gemma Fielding (12)
Lavington Comprehensive School

My Cat

Awaking from her cosy bed,
Waiting to be fed,
When she smells her delicious food,
She jumps upon the side to eat it.

She scampers from room to room
And she decides to sit down.
Then she sees this big, yellow thing,
Pop! It was a balloon.

She then decides to go into the lounge
And sees the curtains.
She starts to climb up them,
Miaow! She fell.

What should she do next?
She knows,
She goes and sees her friend Rex
So off she goes.

When it's time to come in,
It's time for her tea,
But before she comes in she sees a bee.
She ignores it.

When it's time for bed,
She goes in her room,
Lays down
And has a snooze.

Amy Flower (12)
Lavington Comprehensive School

Why Them?

Out of all the things that could happen
No one could prepare for this
Thousands of lives were shattered
Millions of lives at risk

The plane crashed into the tower
Like a knife to bread
Phone calls were made from the plane
To tell their loved ones that would remain

As the dust settled after a few days
All that was left were
Scenes of destruction, shattered glass
With people screaming and crying

'Why did it happen to us?' they say
What really was the point?
Why were they so cruel?
They are the questions we ask

Children now without parents
All because of people
People who are evil
It will always remain a mystery

All that we can say is
It will never happen again
It was terrible and awful
The tragedy will go on!

Emma Fruen (12)
Lavington Comprehensive School

A Poem About Motocross

Was a Saturday morning and all was boring,
Until I heard scramblers roaring,
Over the hill and on the track,
Spanners and screwdrivers worked and worked.

The scramblers' race was about to start,
So I set off on my great, giant kart.
I went over the hill and to the track,
To see all the bikes looking their best.

The race set off with a great, giant *bang!*
The wheel gates went down with a clang.
Some bikes caught some air,
Others went on the table top.

Before I knew the track was bare
And all the scramblers were over there.
My hero had won
So I set off home on my great, giant kart.

Alex Morrison (12)
Lavington Comprehensive School

D-Day

The landing craft speeds towards a sandy hell
The men within her bowels cower in fear
They clutch their guns tightly
For they'll fight against the almighty
All ready to give their lives for their countries

The craft hit the beach and the gates drop down
The men run out getting totally mowed down
Blood and guts are flying
Dying men are crying
Knowing that they'll never go home again

In a matter of hours all is silent
The beach is littered with bodies
But a lone man stood in the middle of it all
And that lone man was me.

Sean Brackstone (13)
Lavington Comprehensive School

WAR!

All the soldiers going to war,
Walking all in line,
All the soldiers walking along,
Marching all in time.

Back at home peace and quiet,
Until the siren sounds,
The Germans fly overhead,
And everyone's running around.

'Attack!' shouts the captain,
So all the soldiers charge,
Cannons going off left and right,
And then a pause as they recharge.

Back at home wives cry,
As lots of husbands die,
Bullets fly everywhere,
As lots of people die.

Many people are injured,
And all the hospitals are packed,
People fighting on the battlefield,
With guns upon their back.

John Dibble (13)
Lavington Comprehensive School

FRIENDS

I like Lilly, little Lilly Lee,
I like Lilly and Lilly likes me.
Lilly likes lemonade, lollipops and lime drops,
I like Lilly, little Lilly Lee.

Lilly lives in Shanghai
And she owns a hi-fi.
Her dad has a black eye from an angry damselfly.
Her mum is a spy employed by Tsinghai,
Her brother is able to fly up in the sky.

I hate Henry, huge Henry Hee,
I hate Henry and Henry hates me.
Henry hates homework, history and hopscotch,
I hate Henry and Henry hates me.

Henry lives at Sendai not far from Kasai,
His dad is a Rabbi and he wears a neck tie.
His mum makes a pot-pie, in it is a magpie,
His sister can be work-shy but she loves those
French fries.

I play with Peter, pretty Peter Pee,
I play with Peter and Peter plays with me.
Peter plays with Pauline, Penny and Patrick,
I play with Peter, pretty Peter Pee.

Peter is a Masai and he comes from Weihai,
His dad comes from Dubai, his nickname is Greenfly.
His mum has been mummified
But still eats a pork pie,
His sister is a pigsty or so they say.

Amy Williams (12)
Lavington Comprehensive School

SPRING

The sun rises from the horizon
And the rain departs.
The birds are singing.

The birds lay eggs
And the people put out their pegs.
The children are playing.

The cows have calves,
The children start to laugh
And the birds are singing.

The fires die down,
The trees are brown
And the children are playing.

The days commence lengthening,
The rain dries through to a slow trickle
And come to a halt.

The sun arises from a distant place
And the rain departs.
The birds lay eggs
And the people put out their pegs.

The cows have calves,
The children begin to laugh.
The fires die down,
The trees are brown.

So the birds commence singing
And the children begin playing.
This is to let us know
That *spring* is here.

Alex Potter (13)
Lavington Comprehensive School

TRAGEDY!

It started as a normal day,
Adults working, children at play,
Grandparents knitting, cars racing,
Babies crying, people arguing.

Instantaneously the aeroplane struck,
I looked and suddenly a great ball of fire ran
Through the building and *yuck!*
People running, people screaming, people crying,
People jumping from the world above,
Some even lost the one they love.

The buildings we talk about are the Twin Towers,
The death toll hits 5000 at the 9th hour,
The buildings fell, there's nothing much more to tell
Except . . .

The fire brigade who were brave and treacherous,
And waded through the rubble were numerous,
To save office workers and passers-by was their job,
But nothing could have prepared them for this
Awful mob.

The world became silent,
Tears were cried,
Some were violent,
Some lied.

My sad tale has now come to an end,
All that is left to say is . . .
That we are ready to *defend.*

Christina Ruddle (12)
Lavington Comprehensive School

Leo

Leos are faithful,
Loving and bold.
Shine like the sun,
Red, yellow, orange and gold.

Our day is Sunday,
The lion my star,
The flower gladioli,
Leos know who they are.

Long, lashing mane,
Their courage is strong,
Working hard,
I'm never wrong.

Warm and loyal,
Generous and fun,
The element of fire,
The lion and sun.

The centre of attention,
Numbers five and nine,
I will reach my goal,
And feel just fine.

A Leo, that's me,
And what about you?
Between July and August,
Just for us two.

Victoria Pike (13)
Lavington Comprehensive School

MORNINGS

When my alarm clock starts to ring,
I whack it on the top.
I wish that school was much later
'Cause I get in a strop.

My bed is warm and cosy,
I want to go to sleep,
But no, I have to go to school
And that I can't delete.

I have a stretch, I rub my eyes,
At least now I'm awake.
I have a yawn, I feel so tired,
Oh no I'm gonna be late!

I run down the stairs
And grab some toast,
My mum sees me awake.
'Mike it's still the weekend
And it's only half-past eight!'

I check the date and climb upstairs
I can't believe it's Sunday!
My clock was wrong,
My bed I long,
I thought today was Monday!

Jennifer Herniman (13)
Lavington Comprehensive School

HALLOWE'EN

A time when witches cast their spell,
A time when evil is let out from Hell,
A time when wolves cry and howl,
A time when black cats start to prowl.

A time when bats fill the sky,
A time when children eat pumpkin pie,
A time when people are raised from the dead,
A time when evil awakens in dread.

A time when vampires' fangs are best,
A time when big spiders are a pest,
A time when ghosts haunt everywhere,
A time when monsters go out to scare.

A time when pumpkins flick and glow,
A time when the graveyard is no place to go,
A time when broomsticks aren't used to clean,
A time when UFOs are always seen.

A time when the moon is as round as can be,
A time when owls hoot with glee,
A time when every nightmare comes true,
A time when the Devil comes to visit you.

Of course, none of it's genuine.

Katie Hart (13)
Lavington Comprehensive School

Leo

Leo was the strangest pet,
My first pet and he had to be strange.
Of course he's strange,
All he is, is a ball of fluff
With two little eyes!
I suppose in a way he's special.
I wake up every morning
And it seems like he's doing
An exercise routine!
His sharp claws gripping each bar of his cage
At lunchtime
You could give him a knife and fork.
After all, he would know how to use them.
His sharp little teeth make it sound like
He is saying hello!
Even my friends think it's funny how
When you come into the room,
He squeaks and waves his little paws at you!
I think he is quite intelligent really,
Especially as he knows his thirteen times table!
Even my brother, who is 16, can't do it,
Well, not as quick as Leo!
He can do good acrobatics too!
Leo does handstands and cartwheels!
Is there no end to my winking, beady-eyed
Quite amazing fluffy lump?
Leo, my (very) amazing
Chinchilla!

Michelle Southey (13)
Lavington Comprehensive School

The Day The World Changed

It started as a normal morning,
Birds were singing, workers yawning,
And little did they know that soon
They'd walk into the towers of doom.

For a passer-by at 9.15,
A most horrific sight they'd see,
A hijacked plane hurtling through the sky
About to destroy six thousand lives.

A crash, and smoke, and flames of fire
The sound of screaming voices, dire.
Some people who knew they'd lose their lives,
Sent calls of love to husbands and wives.

Everybody in complete despair,
No terrorist attack could ever compare
To the heartache and destruction it caused
And for three minutes the whole Earth paused.

Another attack on the second tower,
Both had fallen within the hour,
Leaving a scene of devastation
And broken hearts in every nation.

How could anyone feel such hate,
To put in danger the whole world's fate?
Why did those people want to kill,
When all others want is peace and free will?

Tamzin Jones (14)
Lavington Comprehensive School

Moving House

Cardboard boxes,
Dirty teacups,
Flaking paintwork,
Abandoned toys,
Grubby corners,
Sweaty workmen,
Naked windows,
All bare light bulbs,
Empty sockets,
Moving house!

Unpacked tea chests,
Brand new beakers,
Glossy paint job,
Lively playroom,
Spotless bedroom,
Happy driver,
Full length curtains,
Candelabra,
Whistling kettle,
Moved house!

Ashley Gumbrell (13)
Lavington Comprehensive School

Looking Out Of My Window

I sit on the ledge
Staring out of the window
Watching the rain fall

I sit on the ledge
Staring out of the window
Watching the sun shine

I sit on the ledge
Staring out of the window
Watching the snow melt

I think to myself
If this weather had not come
We wouldn't be here.

Hannah Mason (12)
Lavington Comprehensive School

MANCHESTER UNITED

Man United are the best,
They can beat all the rest.
They've won the double,
They've won the treble,
When they were in a lot of trouble.

It's down to the players if they lose,
When they come off they get some boos.
Sir Alex Ferguson is the manager now,
But soon he'll be throwing in the towel.

Roy Keane is so tough,
And Dennis Irwin has had enough.
David Beckham is superb,
He will score from the curb.

Old Trafford is their ground,
It's the biggest known around.
United are the team for me,
I always watch them on TV.

Lee Michael John Martin (13)
Lavington Comprehensive School

THE MANY DEATHS OF A MOLE

In this world live the moles,
The funny little creatures who burrow down in holes.
For a mole, life is always a danger,
Not just from a tall, dark stranger.
They're blind, so don't know what's ahead,
And that's why they usually end up dead.
An old lady with a lawn mower,
Not being careful of what she runs over.
The little moles keep poppin' up,
Only to get a drastic chop.
Angry men place traps all over,
Trying to kill a mole or gopher.
This little mole is rather dumb,
And ends up dead, sliced through the tum.
Why did the mole cross the road?
To get flattened by a heavy load.
A steamroller on its daily drive,
Squashed the mole at half-past five.
A teenager doing his daily chore,
Was digging holes, what a bore.
The spade slides through the soil with ease,
And into the mole with a squish and a squeeze.
So remember moles when you are working,
Because there's usually one lurking.
When digging, mowing, driving, drilling,
Be careful that you're not killing,
Our funny, furry little friend,
Who normally meets an untimely end.

Liam Davis (13)
Lavington Comprehensive School

A Skater's Tale

Toymachine, Element, Zoo York or Zero,
The choice of decks goes on,
Bearings such as Hawks and Luckys,
Are considered as number one.

The deck I chose was Toymachine,
The trucks are called Tensors,
For bearings I went for Speed Demons,
My parents thought I was senseless.

The feel, the rush as I climb on my board,
My wheels and I are as one,
We take up the challenge,
It may be a day before the tricks are done.

A half-pipe is heaven when I skate on it,
True judgement and skill is all you need,
With luck on my side and wind in my hair,
I'm sure to skate on it with speed.

Before we move on I must mention the gear,
To be a dude on your board,
Calvin Klein would not be fine,
You must have Blind jeans in your hoard.

Tricks of the trade are kickflips and grinds,
Ollies and indys are too,
A true pro can do any of these,
But I can do just a few.

Matthew Gabb (12)
Lavington Comprehensive School

THE BEAST

I was awoken by roaring
I didn't think it was true, but now I believe it, like you should too.
I had heard the myths, so now it's time
to go to the cliffs and make him mine.
I was the only slayer, there was nobody else,
They didn't want to know, they didn't want to help.
So I was on my way with weapons of all kinds,
I was scared, but I tried to block it out of my mind.
I got higher up the cliff and it started to pour with rain,
I was on my own, nobody else came.
There was then another roar,
Which echoed through the mountainous area,
As I got closer it was a lot more scarier.
I walked towards the sound and there it was,
The creature which was twenty foot tall, if not above.
It hid in the shadows, but made its move quickly
As it swept its claw towards my body, I had to move swiftly.
The beast's eyes stared at me continuously, watching my every move,
I reached into my pocket and towards the beast I threw a knife.
The beast went to block it, so I stabbed him with my spear,
I could feel the tension, I could feel the fear.
Then he whipped round his sharp tail and hit me in the knee,
But the beast fell to the ground, there were signs of glee.
The beast was dead, there was no more pain,
But if there are any more beasts I will reduce their numbers to zero,
As on this day I was the hero.

Daniel Baker (14)
Lavington Comprehensive School

WHY?

The once great Titans, standing proud,
Symbols of all that's good,
One faceless act of terror,
One cowardly spur of hatred.

What can be said that hasn't?
What can be thought that won't?
The wounds of pain may never heal,
When families have loved and lost.

Religious wars as reason,
Past actions caused all this,
The countries at conflict, the killing cannot exist.

We're told we must look on,
Yet mourn the dead, we do,
Those who sacrificed all they had,
A place in our hearts, for you.

Being still a child,
With little wisdom at all,
My emotions were set at a fury, when life became dismal,
Anger, worry, confusion, but pray for the brave and true.

The inability to comprehend,
The confusion in our lives,
Please answer my simple question,
Why?

Jamie Harris (13)
Lavington Comprehensive School

HOMEWORK

Another piece of homework,
To spoil a perfect day,
Another piece of homework,
That Sir has passed my way.

One more boring essay,
The second one today.
Why, oh why, please tell me why,
They torture us this way.

A bit of French translation,
Some science information,
An algebra equation,
And lots of punctuation.

I've done my graphs,
And further maths,
And now a break for tea.
Then nose back to the grindstone
For ancient history.

Science, maths and English too,
Drama, music, what shall I do?
My hand is getting very sore,
I think homework is such a bore!

Now I've finished - my poem's done,
At last it's time to have some fun.
Off to my PlayStation I head,
Oh no, Mum says it's time for bed!

Daniel Storey (13)
Lavington Comprehensive School

I'd Like To Be

I'd like to be an iguana,
Perfect camouflage,
Hidden in the tropics,
From danger small and large.

I'd like to be a turtle,
Drifting through the sea,
Very slow and steady,
Yes, a turtle I would be.

I'd like to be a snake,
Slithering through the grass,
Without any legs
But still very fast.

I like being individual,
Just me . . . not three,
So I think that I am happy,
Just being me!

Jess Share (13)
Lavington Comprehensive School

Sadness

As the blue lake scrolls underneath
The warm air that the plane is sitting in
Sadness is the knowledge
That you won't return
Until you've weathered the cold alien winter
Of a faraway continent
Deported by tradition,
By necessity.

Rowan Kennedy (17)
Marlborough College

WAR

One small spark and explosions erupted,
Twisted metal piercing brave living wire.
Last breaths were drawn and human lives ended.

One command and by legions they answered.
One by one they were mowed down by gunfire.
One small spark and explosions erupted.

Twitching bodies lay tortured and scarred,
Red rivers flowing back to the lair.
Last breaths were drawn and human lives ended.

Mines ran from fuses that hissed and smoked,
Frightened of burial in mounds of mire.
One small spark and explosions erupted.

The sky turned black and cold fog descended.
Silence remained and then felt was the ire.
Last breaths were drawn and human lives ended.

Officers searched to find any wounded,
But left were only the brave to admire.
One small spark and explosions erupted.
Last breaths were drawn and human lives ended.

Annie Keddie (17)
Marlborough College

LOST IN BLUE

Marine pale from the wide set door,
Set in dark lengths of this passage.
White woman in your empty space,
Feel small in these cobalt walls.
Tracing the blue with now timeless hands,
You're assured of your last security.

Step back and this space is an aqua limbo,
Nervous eternity in these fathomless walls.
Receiving humanity, this new reality,
Unrestless conscience with your blood running blue.

Alex MacDonald (17)
Marlborough College

My Bronze Buffalo

It stood unmoved on the mantelpiece
Covered in dust.
It had been neglected since I'd been away.

I picked it up. It took some effort,
I'd forgotten how heavy it was.
I held it up to my mouth
And blew the dust off it.

Suddenly he came alive.
His pointed horns glistened in the light -
Two lethal prongs.
His metallic smell engulfed me.
I felt overwhelmed.

He had lost none of his magnificence.
His fine-cut muscles along his back
Had an authoritarian presence about them.

I put him back on the mantelpiece;
A faint ring sounded as he made
Contact with the wooden shelf.
It filled my room
And I felt peaceful . . .
Under his control.

Jason Dunford (14)
Marlborough College

Storm

Waves lapping at the edge of the cliff face,
slapping, clashing, bashing against the shore.
The sand is left smooth. My footprints? Not a trace.

The wind howls like a thumping drum bass,
it seems to have sunk to the ocean floor.
Waves lapping at the edge of the cliff face.

The rain lashes down at a raging pace.
I look at the opening sky in awe.
The sand is left smooth. My footprints? Not a trace.

The water foams like a swirl of white lace.
Bolts of lightning light the sky even more.
Waves lapping at the edge of the cliff face.

The see rages in its own time and space.
The gulls swoop high, crying above, caw, caw!
The sand is left smooth. My footprints? Not a trace.

The moon shines dimly in the sky's embrace.
Thunder bolts down with an almighty roar.
Waves lapping at the edge of the cliff face,
The sand is left smooth. My footprints? Not a trace.

Zinka Bozovic (15)
Marlborough College

Light Bulb

Its appearance unlit, unimpressive, faintly ridiculous
Like a skeletal pear
Or a ghostly, bloated water droplet;
Inside it grows like a tiny plant, a metal hair.

But at a click this thing is alive with fire,
Harsh and white, unnatural and ugly,
Sun's broken blood pumping through the thin metal vein,
Burning a pulsing, colourful memory onto your eyes:
Sheer light tamed.

Luke Wilson (16)
Marlborough College

DEPRESSION

You must fight against the dark, fight for light,
At the end of the tunnel there's a ray.
Ignite the darkness, free the light and fight.

There are many paths in search for the light,
Look carefully, before you choose your way.
You must fight against the dark, fight for light.

If you look hard, using adequate sight,
You may, catch a glimpse of the perfect day.
Ignite the darkness, free the light and fight.

If you're alone and see no way that's right,
Try Jesus, the baby born on the hay.
You must fight against the dark, fight for light.

If the ray leaves your view, fight back with might,
If you don't, you won't see another day.
Ignite the darkness, free the light and fight.

Listen to me, then you will see that I am right.
If you do not, then you will surely pay.
You must fight against the dark, fight for light.
Ignite the darkness, free the light and fight.

Edward Legge (14)
Marlborough College

My Deadly Chemistry

Outside people move hurriedly
Blind to who I am.

I continue my deadly chemistry.
What combination makes a perfect cocktail?

I hear the visitor downstairs,
Look around wildly, tense, don't come upstairs, shh.

When they visit me
I shove the equipment under the bed (don't go off . . .).

Go time now, bring the blanket,
Walk slowly, I'm clumsy.

Pray that no one notices
I look too normal.

Plant, run, wait, bang, blast, heat.
I smile my approval.

Harry Palmer (17)
Marlborough College

Jagged

A jagged crack in the glass
reminds me of the wild, winding river beyond the trees.

Behind me a quiet room. Neat, unusual
furniture, once varnished, now blind with dust.

A sudden chilling gust echoes in the hearth
and last red cinders glow bright and then die.

I recall this time last year.
My old dad, smiling his resigned, ancient grin.

Forecast said it would rain later. If the clumsy radio
is to be trusted I should leave.

He knew the forest like his tanned, weathered hand.
I pretend the cold breath of the trees betrays his memory.

Amy Draper (17)
Marlborough College

REQUIEM FOR A TOY SOLDIER

All wrapped up neat in a brown paper parcel;
You sat on my desk and waited,
Waited till I unfolded your smart, creased shroud -
And when I did - by the light of the halogen bulb
You stood strong; musket raised, bayonet bared.

You stood strong; musket raised, bayonet bared -
As the hoards charged upon you daubed in their infantile thumb paint.
Tomahawks hacking through the blood-red sea
And you were felled, like corn in front of a whirling scythe,
Your face crushed, arms bent, body beaten under the feet.

Your face crushed, arms bent, body beaten under the feet
Of one friend too many.
It wasn't his fault, you *were* lying there and it was teatime.
He's gone now. Don't worry - I'm going to bury you properly,
Under the rose bush,
All wrapped up neat in a brown paper parcel.

Mark Wright (16)
Marlborough College

AFTERNOON MUSIC

The afternoon is glazed mottled turquoise,
Like a well-made piece of pottery; in heat
The air is slowly suffocating.

I cannot speak the words I wish to say.
Music is my language, Brahms my feelings,
Poco Adagio are my words this afternoon.

If you could play back to me you would,
And say what you would want to say . . .
What hurts you to say.

The first phrase floats over the sultry afternoon.
All has become heavy; the people are sitting,
Frail, old, attentive. You have your feet up,
And I am pulled down to a D.
Then I am no longer conscious, notes flow,
My fingers move and I am blind to the stave . . .
I have time to think.

I finish,
Not in key . . . too sharp, too hurried.
I will have time to perfect it later.
Now the expectation of the summer has overcome me,
And I burst, like bubbles from champagne
Into a fury of notes. Tripping up as I go
Through the 'Flight of a Bumblebee',
Over the wheat, down to Geneva Lake.

I have taken control of the lower register . . .
A sensible speed, though the thrill has faded.
Silence. Then laughter.

Katyuli Lloyd (16)
Marlborough College

DINOSAUR EGG

I was five at the time,
Young, and still discovering the world,
But this was something I would never forget.
An extraordinary walk on the beach:
Out of the millions,
The millions of pebbles begging to be selected,
I picked this one to be
My dinosaur egg.

It was special,
Its curves more defined.
Its shape: as it had been plucked from the Stone Age.
It was bigger, better than the rest
And I adored it.
It clinked and clonked when I moved it.
But then I picked it up one last time,
Removed it out of the ordinary.

There it sat on my shelf,
Forever in incubation.
It never did hatch, that egg;
And as I grew older,
And the truth grew apparent,
I put it out of my mind.

The dust gradually accumulated.

There it lies still, extinct.

William Lough (14)
Marlborough College

MAN BURNING

Screaming, arms flung madly into the air
While I watch, totally unbelieving.
The putrid stench of burning flesh and hair
Is due to the collapse of the ceiling.
His blue polyester shirt starts to melt
Horribly, as the resins fuse with flesh.
Flames that lick the skeletal face are felt
No longer: the body a lifeless mesh.
The smoking ashes are all that remain,
Spare the odd, charred object: steel watch, a ring,
Shattered mobile. All is not seen again
Under the rubble that was a building.
'What goes around, comes around', wise men tell,
But this attack is a vision of Hell.

Ramsay Lloyd-Dada (18)
Marlborough College

SEA ANEMONE

I feel the surface under my hands,
Smooth and light like a small piece of glass.
I can see that it is delicate, and finger it gently,
Special as something not to be forgotten.

The colour is a shiny red, faded and mellow;
It glistens in the light and reflects off the windows around me.
I found it on the beach a long time ago,
Brought it home and kept it on my desk.

It has become a kind of charm. I hold it
When I want to think about something.
It still smells a little bit of the sea, faded but there.

One day I will forget about it, or it will get lost,
But when that happens I will have moved on:
Grown up, gone.

Olivia Wright (14)
Marlborough College

Leon: Toulouse - Lautrec

Look at these long-legged beauties.
You can't help the rush, the shivers, every time.
Preposterous; improper, I know,
But I came here to feed, dig my teeth
Into something juicy,
Today and yesterday.
'Waiter, a rib-eye steak, please.'

I often wonder if I'll ever feel
Their penniless figures; bathed in light, draped on tables
In the Green Room.
Until I ever do I'm content to watch;
I can imagine.

Overheated by their icy professionalism
I pay. And leave lonely.
But I don't care. Until my return.

Augusta Pownall (16)
Marlborough College

SONNET

Sunshine is brazen, it's sultry and brash,
It's loud and provoking, it sweeps away woe
But to seek such a thing is both senseless and rash -
Its effects do not last, they are only for show.
Rain's but a shower with the power to thrill,
It tears at you, forcing your fears inside out;
It scolds and it stings and it clearly can chill
'Til ousted for good are all worries and doubt.
So sunshine's a party - so good 'til it ends
And rain is purgation - it hurts but it saves
The one when you're young you must always attend,
The other (be warned) is only for the brave.
For sunshine is false; all contrivance and charm,
In plain honest rain shall I find my balm.

Emma Shearn (15)
Marlborough College

CHOCOLAT

Carnival colours dulled by the dark winds,
That sweep from the north through this quiet rural town.
Villagers crowd alongside the event
Happy to let the time pass them by.
Fluttering skirts blow around the legs
Of gossiping women loyally alongside their husbands.
But a stranger and child stand out,
Looks are exchanged, the verdict: ignore.
The last trailers rattle through
And the gathering disappears behind closed doors.
They watch alone, as litter drifts over the cobbles.

Susanna Hudson (15)
Marlborough College

THE FOUR LADIES ON THE BRIDGE

Father at work in the city,
Mother is one, with daughters of three.
The sky is blue, the sun is high.
Three daughters looking down into the shallow river below,
Flowing fast and calm.
Rounded pebbles on the riverbed,
With rainbow trout swimming over.
The midday sun glistens on the clear water.
The mother looks away, longing for her husband.
The wind is heard amongst the trees as branches sway.
The giant willow gleams light green as it reflects.
The whitewashed house shines bright nearby.
The long road is seen turning off into the trees.

Harry Amos (15)
Marlborough College

ARABIA

Intoxicating spices make my nose tingle,
Piled up into vibrant mounds of colour.

The stifling heat in trapped under palm fronds.
Dark eyes gleam through black abayas.

A woman haggles for a length of silk.

The dark-clad figure comes over,
Touches my brother's and my hair. Muttering.

Hurrying off as the evening mosques start,
Leaving us alone, her touch still heavy on my head.

Claire Spolton-Dean (15)
Marlborough College

FOLLOW YOUR DREAMS

Come one, come all, father and son,
My challenge stands to any man.
I'll take on all or just the one,
See if I keep on standing!
If you mock me,
Look down on me,
I will stay standing.
Try to beat me or defeat me,
I will never lay low.
Set 'em up, I'll knock 'em down,
Even if I've got nowhere to go.
One day I'll stand up tall,
Reach my goal,
Live in my house,
Where in my eyes,
I see it - so very large and magnificent.

Alexander Muniesa (12)
St Joseph's RC Comprehensive School, Swindon

THE LONELY RIDE

Riding on the road on a horse called Swift,
Alone all but for the wind in my hair.
Thinking of a girl at the bottom of my heart,
Dreaming of her face so fair.
Light shining bright in the darkness.

As one proud animal, we raced around the bend,
Riding past a fox in his lair.
Thinking of a girl at the bottom of my heart,
Her great beauty is so rare.
Light shining bright in the darkness.

Into the night-cloaked town.
Up to the inn and dismounted from my horse.
Seeing that girl at the bottom of my heart.
For the open road I have no remorse
A shining light at my side.

Robert Morton (12)
St Joseph's RC Comprehensive School, Swindon

PETTY DIFFERENCES

The reason I am different is because I have no taste,
I have no sense of fashion or a model-perfect face.
I don't have gorgeous features and I'm not an ace at sport,
Does this mean I'm peculiar? Well, that's what I've been taught.

Does it really matter if I'm not in all top sets?
That I walk home with my brother and *don't* play the clarinet?
I mean, I'm not retarded but I'm treated like I'm thick,
And jut because I wear large specs, they always take the mick.

I know that I'm not wanted cos the colour of my skin,
Is two shades darker than the rest, and I'm not exactly thin.
Let's face it, if you're not the same, you're weird and stand alone.
Is this the way that things should be? Should everyone be a clone?

It's obvious the world is split, of this I have no doubt,
But will it always be this way; the 'in' group and the 'out'?
Well, who's to say it can't be changed, it could be done, it's true.
But, if at all it can be done, the change must start with *you!*

(The world is not a perfect place, I'm sure you will agree,
So we should all respect each other as equals, that's the key!)

Bethany Brooke (13)
St Joseph's RC Comprehensive School, Swindon

Proud Of Being Different, But Still Sad

Why is this person picking on me?
He doesn't know me
So why is he picking on me?
Is it because I'm different?
Is it because I don't look like him?
Wow! He's as hard as nails and I'm as soft as snow,
But does that honestly matter?
Does that change who I am inside?
No!
I like who I am!
Should I change because he wants me to?
If everyone knew me as I know me,
Everyone would want to be different like me!
I'm proud of who I am
Why should I change?
I'm proud of being different!
More important, I'm proud of being me!

Mark New (13)
St Joseph's RC Comprehensive School, Swindon

Different People

When I go walking down the street,
I see people who I meet.
People who are big, people who are small,
People who are not there at all.

A cool executive on his phone,
A tramp who hasn't even got a home.
Pushing her trolley is the little old dear,
Religions and cultures they're all here.

But now I ask simply myself why?
As they go slowly wandering by.
Different looks and different skins,
It's a better world for us all to live in.

Adrienne Paone (13)
St Joseph's RC Comprehensive School, Swindon

THE WAY WE ARE

'Write a poem about being different!'
Our teacher once did say.
The reason for this is easy -
It's because of DNA.

Mixing up our chromosomes
Gives us our characteristics,
The way we end up turning out
Depends upon statistics.

When Mum and Dad have babies,
Their chromosomes do meet,
Making little miracles,
Which is such a great feat!

All of us are different,
Tall, short, black or white,
But sometimes things go wrong -
Like some people have no sight.

Big bad boils, bumps and bruises,
Facial disfigurements and piles,
Needles as long as snakes,
Keep some people running for miles!

Helen Torrens-Burton (13)
St Joseph's RC Comprehensive School, Swindon

BEGINNING OF THE END

I don't want to leave everything behind,
Will you accept my difference and be kind.
When I look back on my life
At the challenges I've overcome,
The obstacles I have faced
And the tasks I have done

It seems only yesterday I was fighting in the war.
No fault of my own, it was the country's law.

Food is merely a mirage in my mind,
Though even there it is hard to find.
The only thought that keeps people on track,
the will to live, I ask you, 'What's that?'

I pray for the nights when I can lay down and sleep,
And fear the days full of exhaustion and heat.
However hard, I shall miss my past,
Though I do hope this journey shall be my last.

Rosanna Harries (13)
St Joseph's RC Comprehensive School, Swindon

COMPARISONS

Why do they think that I'm to blame?
It's not my fault I'm not the same.
Just because I'm not all normal,
It doesn't make me that abnormal.

Why do they think that I'm so bold?
I don't know what the future will hold.
Why do they think that I don't get hurt?
They just think they can treat me like dirt.

I'll do my best and try to achieve,
And let the rest do what they believe.
If I don't reach their loft crest
They can be sure, *I did my best!*

Sarah Harris (13)
St Joseph's RC Comprehensive School, Swindon

I Am The Same As You!

I am not weird, I am not mad,
I am the same as you,
I may look a mess and smell real bad,
But I am a person just like you.

I am very scruffy; my hair is too long,
I'm not the same as you,
People look at me, like I've done something wrong,
But I'm a person just like you.

I beg for money; I live outdoors,
I'm not the same as you,
My home is the streets; my bed is the floor,
But I am a person just like you.

I don't do drugs; I am not scum,
I am the same as you.
I'm very smart, not at all dumb,
I'm a person just like you.

I don't have a home; I don't have a family,
That's how I'm different from you,
I do have friends; I do have love,
I am a person just like you.

Leanne Cowie (14)
St Joseph's RC Comprehensive School, Swindon

Cold

Who are they to stand and stare
In this land so empty of care?
Here on the streets it is very cold,
To survive here you have to be bold.

Do they think I'm as blind as a bat?
Pointing at me like I'm a dirty smelly rat.
You'll be lucky to get a bath,
The best I've done is a puddle on a path.

All I want is somewhere warm,
Like a friendly youth hostel dorm.
'Hey Mister! Got any dosh?
All I want it for is some warm nosh!'

So, that's my exciting life story,
I know it's not good enough to be on Jackanory.
You are the ones who stand and stare
In this land so empty of care.

Christian Paprocki (13)
St Joseph's RC Comprehensive School, Swindon

Alone

I feel all alone,
In the middle of nowhere,
Even one movement
Gives me a scare.

You really don't want
To see the sight,
When a small little thing
Gives me a fright.

It makes me feel sad
When I'm all on my own.
I get very cold
Like I'm chilled to the bone.

I really don't like it
When there's no one around.
I just want to put
My head in the ground.

David Netley (12)
St Joseph's RC Comprehensive School, Swindon

UNLUCKY LUCKY

Lucky is not lucky any more,
She keeps on scratching at the back door.
No one to let her in, no one to care.
Not loved any more it's not fair.

A Christmas present she had been before,
A fluffy little puppy from the pet store.
Cuddly, playful, lovely, she had a ball.
Then she grew up in no time at all.

Now the children have no time to play,
She must go, she cannot stay.
Like a sad, saggy old toy,
Rejected - no more love and no more joy.

Sarah Jane Withey (13)
St Joseph's RC Comprehensive School, Swindon

LONELINESS

Being lonely is like a dog being treated badly.
It is a sun going through a total eclipse.
It is like a child being murdered so sadly.
It is a blazing fire burning your lips.

You're so scared, alone and terrified.
You fear you're not loved and no one cares.
You feel abandoned, distressed, petrified.
Wishing you were with other children playing
truth or dares.

A child welcomes you and makes you their friend.
You feel loved, happy and secure.
You wish and wish this day won't end
You have found someone you love and adore.

Nicola Cremin (13)
St Joseph's RC Comprehensive School, Swindon

CLAUSTROPHRENIC

I can't wait till I get home
but there's not much to do when you're living alone.
When you're claustrophobic it's not much fun
every day just seems to be glum.

Always looking over my shoulder,
in a tight space I get colder.
Like a dark shadow a bit like rain,
a living hell but I feel no pain.

Sleepwalking's another problem I have
but no one else knows I'm actually mad.
Mum and Dad left for France
maybe one day I'll snap out of this trance.

The tablet I'm on has no effect
My life is full of wholesome regret.
I have no friends, I don't like the phone
I can get used to living on my own.

Matt Mochan (13)
St Joseph's RC Comprehensive School, Swindon

UGLY

I walk down the street, people stare,
Sometimes I look at them with a hurt face,
And sometimes I don't care.

Blistered, bumpy, red-raw cheeks,
As rough as sharp sandpaper,
That won't disappear even in weeks.

I hope and pray that it will go away,
That I'll wake up from a bad nightmare,
But I know it will stay.

One day I'll learn to live with it,
Ignore all those funny looks,
I wish they could fall into a pit.

Michelle Moloney (13)
St Joseph's RC Comprehensive School, Swindon

BEING DIFFERENT

Does it matter if I'm different
Does it matter if I'm me
Why don't you look inside
And not just what you see

Please give me a chance
Before you turn away
Listen to your heart
Then maybe you might stay

Listen to the person
And I'll tell you how I feel
Just put aside your vision
It's not that big a deal

Can't you see I'm hurting
When people turn their backs
I try to open up to them
But they slip away like wax

If I ever find someone
That truly understands
My heart will probably stop
As they take me in their hands

How long will I have to wait
How far will I have to go
Until I've found somebody
Who will love and *always* show.

Nicola Dyer (14)
St Joseph's RC Comprehensive School, Swindon

The Ballad Of Romeo And Juliet

Romeo and Juliet are two young lovers
Who went to a party were they met
But their parents hate each other
So they meet in secret places.

Romeo then says, 'Marry me, be together
Forever and ever till the day that we shall die
And our hearts will live on
And maybe our marriage will bring peace to our families.

So that we can be happy
And not live in secret anymore
And our families can live in peace
So we can be happy.'

But what a bitter end
To the two sweet lovers
As one wakes to find the other dead
So Juliet shoots herself.

But then the parents see what has happened
They make peace.
When the families have made peace
They buried Romeo and Juliet together as they had wished.

So we have come to the end
Of the story of the two sweet lovers
Romeo and Juliet
Who shall never forget.

Samantha Hutchison (12)
The John Bentley School

The Ballad Of Romeo And Juliet

Romeo and Juliet
Were loving someone else
When at the party they both met
Alone like down the wells.
Very soon later
They found out the truth
Enemies like the waiter
Against the very sweet tooth.
After the party, Romeo
Sneaked under Juliet's balcony
Juliet leaned over
Then Romeo said,
'Will you marry me?'
When Juliet agreed
And convinced was the friar
Romeo and Juliet married
Their love went higher and higher.
That night a relative of Juliet's
Killed a friend of Romeo's.
When Romeo heard,
Quicker than a jet he killed Tybalt
Who is now below.
Romeo was banished,
Juliet was sad
She went to the friar and said what she wished.
Juliet's sadness was turned into gladness.
She drank a liquid know as a potion
Which knocked her into a deadly phase.
For forty-eight hours she had a lack of motion.
Forty-eight hours is exactly two days.
Romeo never heard
Except she was dead.
He went to the church
Where she lay on her bed.

Romeo stabbed himself.
When Juliet woke
She saw the knife and stabbed herself
And got buried under a tree of oak.

Antony Spencer (13)
The John Bentley School

THE BALLAD OF ROMEO AND JULIET

Romeo saw a girl
He'd never seen before.
She had a curl in her hair
That knocked Romeo to the floor.

Romeo and Mercutio went to a disco
But Mercutio ordered fries to go.
But Romeo didn't want fries to go
He wanted to stay, so he said, 'No!'

He saw a girl called Juliet
He went to her to say, 'Hey, hey.'
Then Juliet had to go
But Romeo said, 'Don't go!'

Romeo stole Juliet's heart
Even though they were enemies
But the very first time Romeo saw Juliet
They fell in love.

Romeo and Juliet got married in a church
But not a lot of people came
As nobody knew about it.
So Romeo and Juliet got married in a church
with only one witness
Who was the priest.

Leanne Armitage (12)
The John Bentley School

THE BALLAD OF ROMEO AND JULIET

This is the story of two lovers,
Romeo and Juliet.
They will always be there for each other
It's been like that ever since they met.

The story of two lovers,
Whose families were at war.
The ones who have been lovers since they met each other
And now they want even more.

The story of these lovers
Who at last marry in secret
Juliet's father and mother
Wanted Juliet to marry someone they met.

The story of these lovers
All came to an end.
The story of those lovers
Montagues and Capulets then became friends.

Carla Dance (12)
The John Bentley School

THE BALLAD OF ROMEO AND JULIET

Once upon a party Romeo and Juliet became more than just friends.
They promised to love each other till the very end.

They planned to marry in secret away from their friends
And live happily ever after is how some stories end.

They married in a church with hardly anyone around.
Then they parted with their hearts drumming but you could
hear no sound.

When Romeo waited to see his new young love
He made a mistake by being late.

When Romeo cried his last, his wife awoke
But only to behold her dying love Romeo.

At her wits' end she took her lover's gun and parted from this world
Not a sound could be heard only an echo through the church.

Laura Fortey (12)
The John Bentley School

THE BALLAD OF ROMEO AND JULIET

Romeo, oh Romeo
Quick I need a kiss
Quick before I begin to miss!

Carry me off in a beautiful carriage
And off we go to get married.

Juliet, oh Juliet
My beautiful bride
Come to your balcony quick
And off in the night we will ride.

And happy they are
Hand in hand
The Capulets and Montagues
Live happily in their own land.

Romeo and Juliet are laid to sleep
Do you hear our families arguing.
Shh! Not a peep.

Kirsty Spicer (12)
The John Bentley School

ROMEO AND JULIET

Romeo and Juliet, two young lovers,
The only thing is they hated each other's brothers,
They pecked and pecked,
On each other's neck.

Juliet had a servant who is such a dog,
She also had a wicked mum who nearly saw them snog,
In the swimming pool they snog,
But still Romeo is as cool as a toilet bog.

They both met at a party,
Eating a packet of Smarties,
Romeo got chased,
But they couldn't keep up with his pace.

In the end he got caught,
Sent away with his own sort,
But just before he got wed,
But now he's dead.

Paul Herring (12)
The John Bentley School

THE BALLAD OF ROMEO AND JULIET

The Capulets and the Montagues
Were a threat to all.
Romeo and Juliet hate to fall.
But always came again to their love.

For Romeo and Juliet came to all.
Friend and again start to fight.
But they will start to fall in love
Because it was love at first sight.

All the poison was drunk
Romeo had no cause.
Juliet woke up
And all was the end.

Shaun Noble (12)
The John Bentley School

The Ballad Of Romeo And Juliet

I'm gonna tell you the story
Of Romeo and Juliet,
One was a Montague who made it all gory,
They had a feud with the Capulets.

The party at the Capulets,
Romeo was there.
He saw Juliet in the corner,
And had an almighty long glare.

They met each other secretly,
They got married while they were still alive.
Juliet wanted peace and harmony,
Romeo said, 'We will survive!

Now go or you'll be dead,
Do not come back
Or they'll cut off your head
They might even put you in a sack.'

'Romeo I'm in the church,
I'm not really dead now.
Come and find me, please search.
Don't leave me now.'

Matthew Edwards & Ashley Miller (12)
The John Bentley School

The Ballad Of Romeo And Juliet

Romeo and Juliet
Were two young lovers
Who hated each other's brothers.

They begged and begged
To be with each other
So they asked the friar
To let them get married.

The friar was hoping
There would be peace
But the friar was wrong
So the feud continued.

Romeo was shocked to find Juliet dead,
So he killed himself with poison.
Then Juliet killed herself because Romeo was dead.

Daniel Bennett (12)
The John Bentley School

The Sound Of War

I know a person
And that person was in a house.
Their house was bombed, but that person
Still lies there breathing.
The house has gone
And now the sky is scarlet red.

Bombs are blasting.
I can hear the sounds of war,
I hear people screaming,
People running,
People crying.

The person is still,
Breathing slowly,
The person stands up,
They scream and run, out into
The sounds of war, war, war.

Kim Kenyon-Noquet (11)
The John Bentley School

The Ballad Of Romeo And Juliet

Romeo and Juliet were at a party
Started swinging
Started getting arty
Until the party stopped.

They secretly got married
And off they carried
With a beautiful
White and gold carriage (not).

Romeo, Romeo he did a crime,
He killed my baby cousin
You are so divine.
So please can you still stay
But you will pay
For the crime that you committed.

The couple's love ended
When they thought it would last.
It finished with a kiss
Which was their everlasting wish
Of being together at last.

Samantha White (12)
The John Bentley School

SUMMER

Summer, summer in the air,
You can smell it everywhere.
You can see flowers all around,
Popping up out of the ground.
Children playing in the sun,
Having lots and lots of fun.
Buzzy bees take pollen from the trees,
So children can ask, 'Can we have some honey please?'
The sun comes out and starts the day,
Some time in the month of May.
Birds start cheeping a lovely song,
Maybe short, maybe long.
Time to camp out, have some fun,
Hop, skip, jump and run.

Georgine Dunwell (11)
The John Bentley School

EAR-SPLITTING

E veryone is
A nnoyed when I
R ush about

S houting, so I
P ounce and be
L oud.
I love
T o
T otally
I rritate loads of
N utty
G randads.

Emily Tanner (11)
The John Bentley School

ME

L ittle am I
I watch TV
T omato I hate
T oboggan in the snow
L ove playing computer games
E at a bit.

Kaden Fillis (11)
The John Bentley School

FRIENDLY

F unny and always happy
R eady to be welcoming
I 'm helpful and kind
E very day I play with my friends
N ot mean and nasty
D on't ignore my friends
L ike helping people
Y ou'll always see me being friendly.

Emma Austin (11)
The John Bentley School

PRETTY

P leased to see you
R eliable in class
E veryone
T alk to me
T ell me what your name is
Y elling, playing games.

Abigail Taylor (11)
The John Bentley School

THE BALLAD OF ROMEO AND JULIET

It all started at a party,
The party got out of hand.
Romeo likes to love and be arty,
They kissed in the middle of the band.

They killed Romeo's best friend,
Then Romeo started crying.
He made his best friend's life end,
This left Romeo sighing.

Then Romeo killed Tybalt,
Because of his anger.
Saying that it was all Tybalt's fault,
People said Romeo was a good angel.

Romeo came to see Juliet,
He felt that Juliet was dead.
Romeo said that he was a good threat,
Because Juliet was lying sound on her bed.

Juliet woke up to see Romeo,
He had already drunk the poison.
Romeo had put on a bad show,
This left Juliet in a bad situation.

James Elliott (12)
The John Bentley School

SWIRLING

Through the oceans,
Dolphins turning,
Through the seas,
Whales swirling.

Over the waves
Fish jumping,
Under the coral,
Shrimps thumping.

Emma Jones (11)
The John Bentley School

The Ballad Of Romeo And Juliet

The families, the Montagues and Capulets
They are fighting all the time
They fight until they get fat lips
But Romeo and Juliet always turn out fine.

Romeo killed Tybalt so he fell down dead
Oh what had Romeo done
There was blood everywhere, was Tybalt dead?

Romeo was now banished
So he ran away
Romeo had gone so far, now he was famished
What became of him that day?

Juliet drank a potion to awake in forty-eight hours
Then Friar Lawrence sent a note
Juliet then woke covered in flowers
Romeo heard the news that Juliet was dead
So he went to fetch his coat.

That is the end of this tragic tale
Romeo killed himself
Juliet had woken up and gave a wail
She saw the gun and shot herself.

Laura Fairbrass (12)
The John Bentley School

THE BALLAD OF ROMEO AND JULIET

This is a story of Romeo and Juliet
They both met at a party and fell in love
Their love was like a jet.
Then Romeo died and Juliet died
They both fell dead.

The story goes that the two lovers go
Like the trees in the wind blow
But Romeo goes to the house of his foes.

Then Romeo goes to meet with Juliet
But Romeo scared Juliet, that was dim
And Juliet screams like a trondon bagget
They grabbed each other and fell and swim.

Seconds later their heads popped out of the pool
And gasped for air.
They said they'd get married which was cool
And Romeo ran like a baby bear.

They got married in a private church.
His friend died on a sandy beach.
he killed a man like a broken up carriage
Then he ran away like a bullet that hit a peach.

Juliet drank a potion that made her dead
But this was a trick to get her love.
Romeo drank some poison then hit his head
Juliet in one blast came down like a glove.

Kevin Square (12)
The John Bentley School

The Ballad Of Romeo And Juliet

Romeo and Juliet
Went to a party
They couldn't take their eyes off each other
When they met.

'May I marry Juliet,' Romeo said
The vicar said, 'No, but I'll get you together
But don't wake her, she's in bed.'
Romeo said, 'I want her forever.'

Romeo finds out his friend's dead
He starts to cry and shouts.
He gets a gun, shoots Tybalt in the head
Without a doubt.

He gets bound from the cops
And goes to the desert
But there's hardly any crops,
Then his postman Bert

Pats the post in the mailbox
But Romeo never read it,
About Juliet was dead but not the pox
He went to the church,
The candles were lit.

He sees Juliet lying down dead
As he kisses her she wakes,
Romeo takes poison and kills himself
And he says his last words.

Mark Ducker (12)
The John Bentley School

THE BALLAD OF ROMEO AND JULIET

Romeo and Juliet met in a crowd at a party
and they were proud.
They kissed in a lift then got a big gift
But they realised it wasn't to last.

Her mother is a bit of a witch and took Juliet to her dad,
Her dad said, 'Hey, I just want to say, I think you're a bit of a babe!'

Romeo looked sad, no wonder why,
His love was a Capulet and he was so shy
Because he is a Montague, she was so hated by the rest of his crew.

At the end, death came between the two lovers who were so keen.
The families realised they were so stupid
To keep these two lovers being hit by Cupid.

Alex Cook (12)
The John Bentley School

BIZARRE

B ewildered most of the time
I dle nearly all the time
Z any I am
A ccident-prone
R eally freaky
R emarkably ridiculous
E ating I enjoy.

Jake Oliver (11)
The John Bentley School

THE BALLAD OF ROMEO AND JULIET

The Montagues and Capulets hate each other,
In a gas station they met,
In haste one shot the other,
This was an event neither family would forget.

Romeo sneaked into a party,
And found to his delight
He found fair Juliet looking a bit tarty,
And it was love at first sight.

The families fought once more,
And Mercutio died,
Romeo shot Tybalt to the floor
And then Juliet cried.

Romeo got banished from the city,
And stayed in a caravan,
Thinking of his pretty
He went out and missed the mail man.

Romeo heard that Juliet was dead
And then he went straight to her,
Then he drank poison and then he was dead,
Juliet woke and cried but there was no cure.

Juliet shot herself in the head,
The two families stopped fighting,
Because their two youngest children were dead,
Then they all started crying.

Daniel Hawkins (13)
The John Bentley School

BALLAD OF ROMEO AND JULIET

Romeo fell in love that night
To a girl called Juliet
It almost caused a fright
But he hadn't even kissed yet

That night after the party
He crept in over the wall
He remembered Juliet was all tarty
And fell into the pool.

Romeo started to swim
He heard the guards coming
Then Juliet jumped in
They were singing and humming

He kissed Juliet on the lips
About four times
Then started to fiddle with her bits
It came to the end of their time.

Leif Hadfield (12)
The John Bentley School

THE COUNTRYSIDE AND THE CITY

The countryside
I travelled through the countryside
And saw a nice calm sky
Cows mooing
Horses neighing
Pigs snorting
Potatoes being picked by hand

The city
Is noisy
The sky is black
Cars brumming
Exhaust pipes blowing
No farms
No countryside.

Mary Webb (11)
The John Bentley School

THE BALLAD OF ROMEO AND JULIET

At first look they fell in love.
The families hated the sight of the other.
Romeo thought Juliet was an angel from above.
Romeo thought Juliet had a crazy mother.

'Romeo, Romeo where for art thou Romeo'.
Romeo was near the pool.
Juliet loves Romeo so.
She thinks he's really cool.

Romeo gets banished because he murdered Juliet's cousin.
Juliet cries for her love.
Juliet's family thought Romeo had done a big sin.
Romeo flies to Juliet's side like a dove.

Friar Lawrence gives her something to sleep for forty-eight hours.
Romeo thinks she is dead.
He loves Juliet so he doesn't live anymore.
Juliet lies dead on her bed.

Bryony Salmon (12)
The John Bentley School

THE BALLAD OF ROMEO AND JULIET

Romeo and Juliet loved each other.
But the Capulets and Montagues hated each other.
But Juliet's loud-mouthed mother didn't know
Nor did the father.

Romeo and Juliet wanted to be together
But Juliet's nursemaid told her he was a Capulet
But their love was as light as a feather
Still I can't believe he didn't tell her
I wanted to fire him out a cannon.

The scary mother was ugly
Juliet's father hurt her.
He was so bugly
Romeo broke her heart by dying.

Romeo, Romeo sat on the wall
Romeo fell in the pool.
Being pushed off a molehill
While her mother went to get some wool.

Joanne Bright (12)
The John Bentley School

THE BALLAD OF ROMEO AND JULIET

It happened like a gift
He followed around.
They made love in a lift
Until she pinned him to the ground.

They had a fight
They punched and they thumped
Then Tybalt had a fright
Until the blood started to pump

Romeo was horrified
That his friend was dead
Romeo was so terrified
He pulled the trigger to Tybalt's head

Romeo was banished to a far away place
And Tybalt is dead in his coffin bed
Then Romeo found his base
Juliet is dead, he hoped he would lose his head.

Adrian Curtis (13)
The John Bentley School

The Ballad Of Romeo And Juliet

The Montagues and Capulets fighting it out
Evil against evil, they fight day by day
Also without a doubt
They kill during May.

They stay until they were troubled
Romeo never knew his true love
Until he said a load of mumble
And saw a pure dove.

Mercutio what a bloke
Romeo's best friend joined together in might
Tybalt was killed and soaked
Tybalt before got Mercutio at sight.

'Romeo, Romeo where for art thou Romeo?' cried Juliet
Romeo and Juliet marry, death do us part
Juliet drinks a remedy, Romeo kills himself
Just after they met
Juliet then shot herself, oh thou art.

Adam Johnson (12)
The John Bentley School

Romeo And Juliet

Romeo and Juliet had love at first sight,
They saw each other as much as they could every night,
To see each other was one big fight,
And all they wanted to do was to put it right.

The innocent love that they thought they had,
Everyone else thought it was definitely bad.
Each precious moment they had together
They thought it should last forever and ever.

It wasn't to be, the thought of being apart,
Cut though their innocent youthful hearts,
Their hearts were breaking, they did not want it to end,
For their love he will try to defend.

But the families were to win, breaking them apart,
Not realising this was the start.
The end was so final, the love they showed
Was to last a lifetime. Their lifetime.

Samantha Trollope (12)
The John Bentley School

The Ballad Of Romeo And Juliet

Romeo sees Roselyn
Juliet is a pretty girl that he will never forget
He thinks oh she's mine.
He doesn't know if he's gonna regret.

Romeo has spotted some pie
He sees something he'll never forget
But something else has caught his eye
Her name is Juliet.

Juliet has spotted Romeo
Juliet ate some apple pie
'Oh he's mine too,' said Juliet
So this is sour and very sweet pie.

Romeo and Juliet are in love
Juliet is truly in love with Romeo
Romeo thinks Juliet is like a dove
She clearly loves him so.

Kimberley Brown (12)
The John Bentley School

THE BALLAD OF ROMEO AND JULIET

'Romeo, Romeo where for art thou Romeo'
Romeo's sat down again, still waiting.
He loved Roselyn so.
He's now very tired of dating.

Something has caught Romeo's eye
Juliet's lips are as red as strawberries.
Her perfume smells like his favourite pie
And her eyes are like bulging blueberries.

Romeo stands under a light,
'Oi, Juliet do you fancy a date?
But I'll meet you by the cemetery gate.'

Romeo is so excited,
He's getting ready for his date
He's going out with Juliet and he's delighted
But Juliet hasn't turned up yet
So he'll have to wait.

Sara Jones (13)
The John Bentley School

THE BALLAD OF ROMEO AND JULIET

This is the story of two lovers, Romeo and Juliet.
They will always be there for each other,
It's been like that since they've met.

The story of two lovers, whose families were at war,
The ones who have been in love since they've met
Each other, and now they want even more.

The story of these lovers, who at last marry in secret,
Juliet's father and mother wanted Juliet to marry
Someone they met.

The story of these lovers all comes to an end
The story of those lovers, Montagues and Capulets
Then become friends.

Kathryn Mansell (12)
The John Bentley School

THE BALLAD OF ROMEO AND JULIET

Monagues and Capulets hate each other,
Even though Romeo and Juliet love each other
Monagues and Capulets aren't a equal line,
But Romeo and Juliet are fine.

Romeo and Juliet got married,
Romeo and Juliet went in a carriage,
Even though it was a secret,
Everyone had to keep it.

Romeo had killed a Capulet,
Then he had to run away,
Romeo said goodbye to Juliet
And said he would come back another day.

Juliet's heart had stopped its beating
Romeo thought this life was done,
He remembered back to their first meeting
His grieving heart was overcome.

Jessica Evans (12)
The John Bentley School

THE BALLAD OF ROMEO AND JULIET

As Romeo entered the party of the Capulets
He saw not the one he wanted to see
No not the beauty Rosalind
But behind the tropical fish tank
Our Romeo saw a jewel too valuable to price.

This was no ordinary jewel
No, this jewel was dangerous,
This jewel was Juliet Capulet.

For every night they did meet
And for every night our Romeo
Was getting forever in danger
Of being discovered.

Jack Smith (12)
The John Bentley School

My Journey

In Kent
a wide farmhouse
with animals
quiet and peaceful
so you can hear
birds call to one another
in the middle of summer.

Horses neighing
cows mooing
and dogs barking
in the middle of summer.

The scenery carries
on forever, and
no motors in sight
in the middle of summer.

Dogs running free
and rabbits running
through the grass
in the middle of summer.

Only a tractor
carrying some
hay bales
in the middle of summer.

Sally Webb (11)
The John Bentley School

ROMEO AND JULIET

Romeo and Juliet
Loved one another
They met one another,
Through a fish tank cover.

Romeo and Juliet
Kissed on the balcony
For the first time ever
But Juliet's mother caught them kissing one another.

Romeo and Juliet's
Families hated one another
But they kept their love a secret
Until their families found out about their love for one another.

Romeo and Juliet's
Love was found out
They both killed one another
As they thought it was the only way they could stay together.

Romeo and Juliet's
Families felt very sad
So they decided to make up
And forget all the bad.

Lucy Carter (12)
The John Bentley School

THE BALLAD OF ROMEO AND JULIET

Romeo loved Juliet
Since the day that they met
They found out they loved each other
But kept the secret from her mother

Romeo climbed up the wall
But he slipped
Fell in the pool

Romeo said
'I love you so
Let's get wed'
'OK let's go'

So off to church
They did trot
To see the vicar
And tie the knot

An introduction made to Paris
But Juliet was too embarrassed
To tell her mum that she had wed
Romeo the groom instead

Juliet was very sad
An argument she had with Dad
A potion then she would drink
Romeo said, 'She's dead, I think'.

He could not stand it any longer
The potion he took was much stronger
When she awoke she found him dead
Then shot herself in the head.

Hayley Wiggins (12)
The John Bentley School